FOR ORGANS, PIANOS & ELECTRONIC KEYBOARDS

E-Z PLAY® TODAY

45

Love Ba

2nd Edition

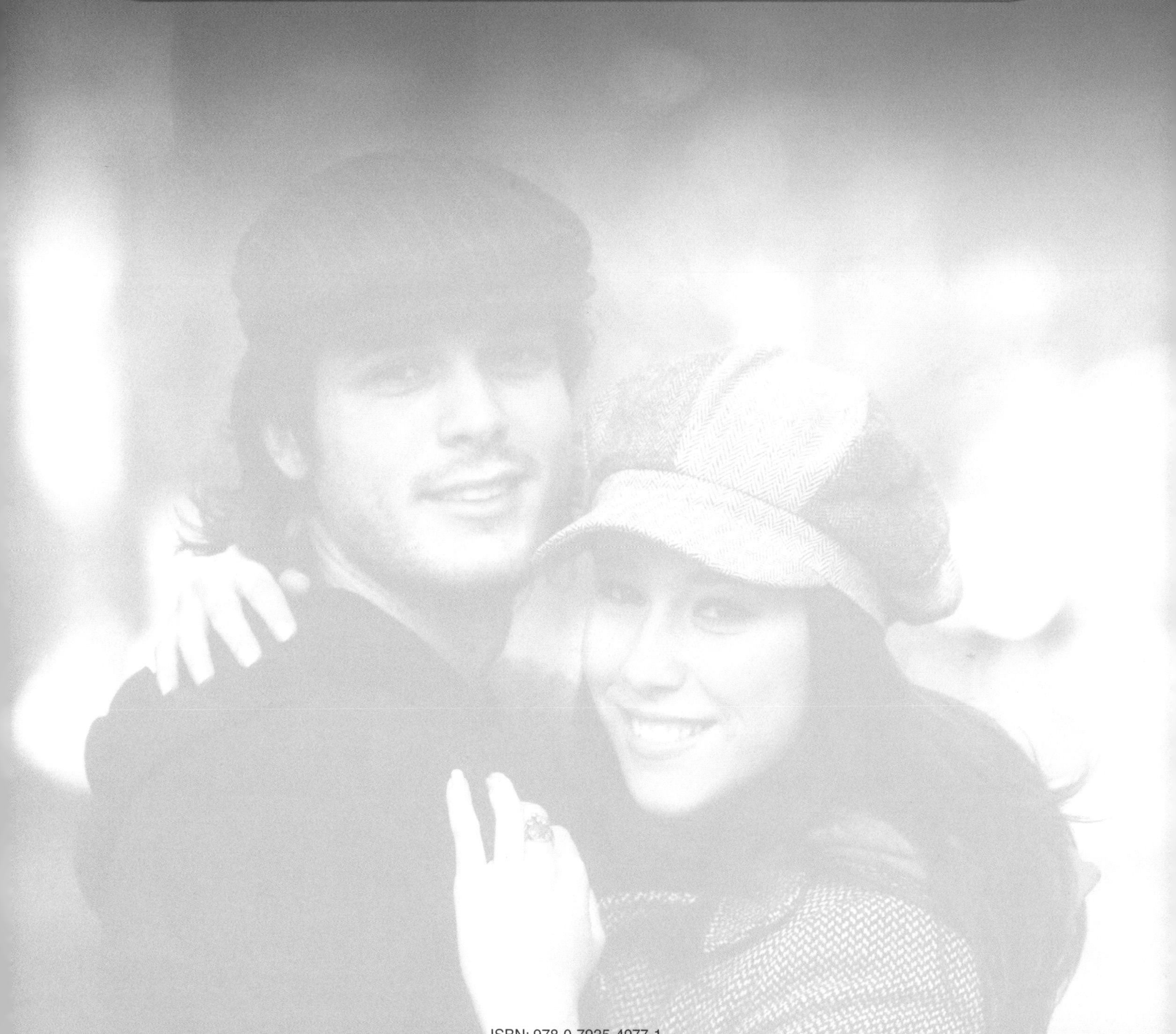

ISBN: 978-0-7935-4977-1

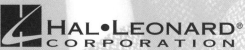

HAL•LEONARD® CORPORATION

7777 W. BLUEMOUND RD. P.O. BOX 13819 MILWAUKEE, WI 53213

Visit Hal Leonard Online at
www.halleonard.com

Can't Help Lovin' Dat Man

from SHOW BOAT

Registration 5
Rhythm: Ballad or Swing

Lyrics by Oscar Hammerstein II
Music by Jerome Kern

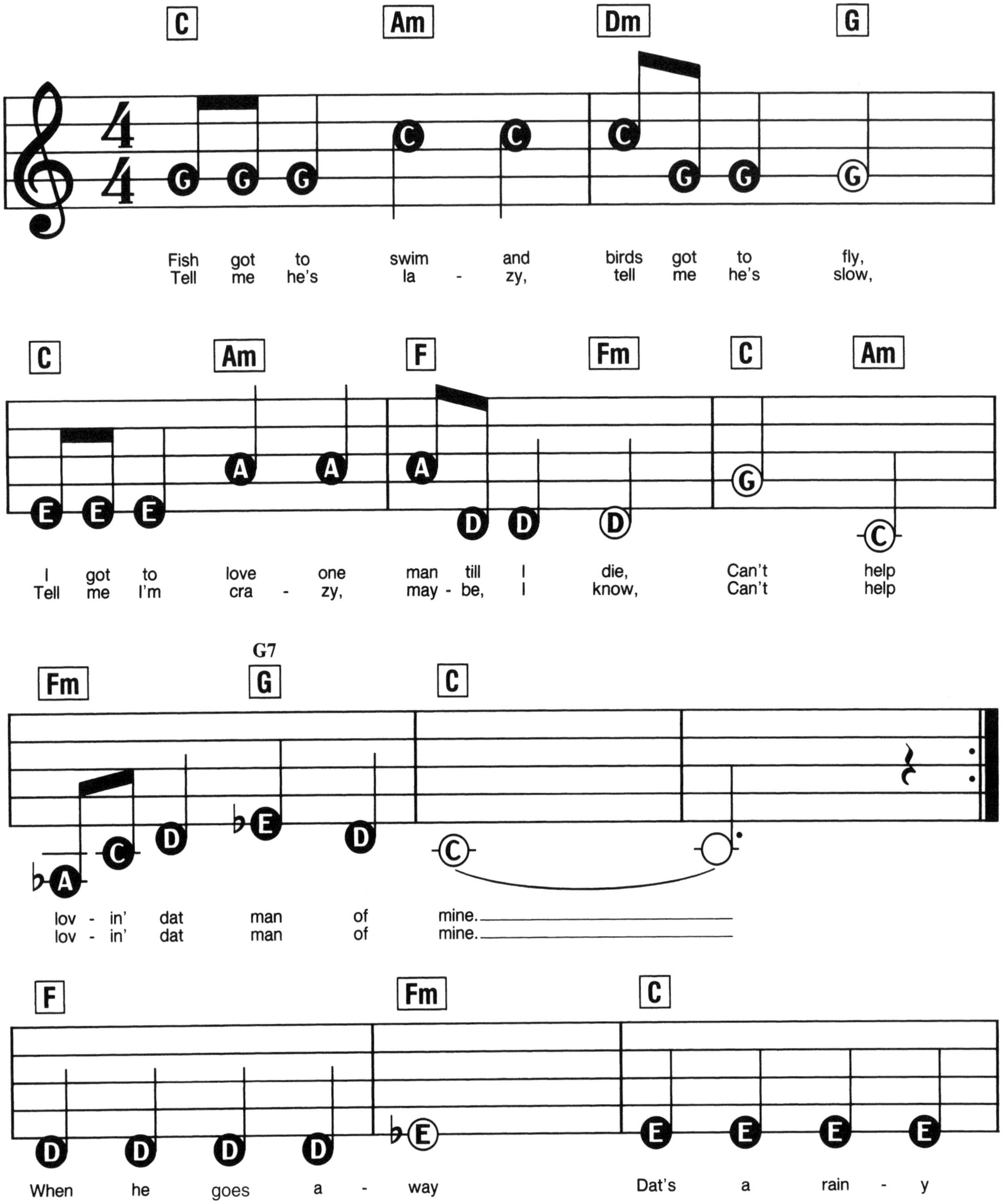
C Am Dm G
Fish got to swim and birds got to fly,
Tell me he's la - zy, tell me he's slow,
C Am F Fm C Am
I got to love one man till I die,
Tell me I'm cra - zy, may - be, I know,
Can't help
Can't help
Fm G7 G C
lov - in' dat man of mine.
lov - in' dat man of mine.
F Fm C
When he goes a - way
Dat's a rain - y

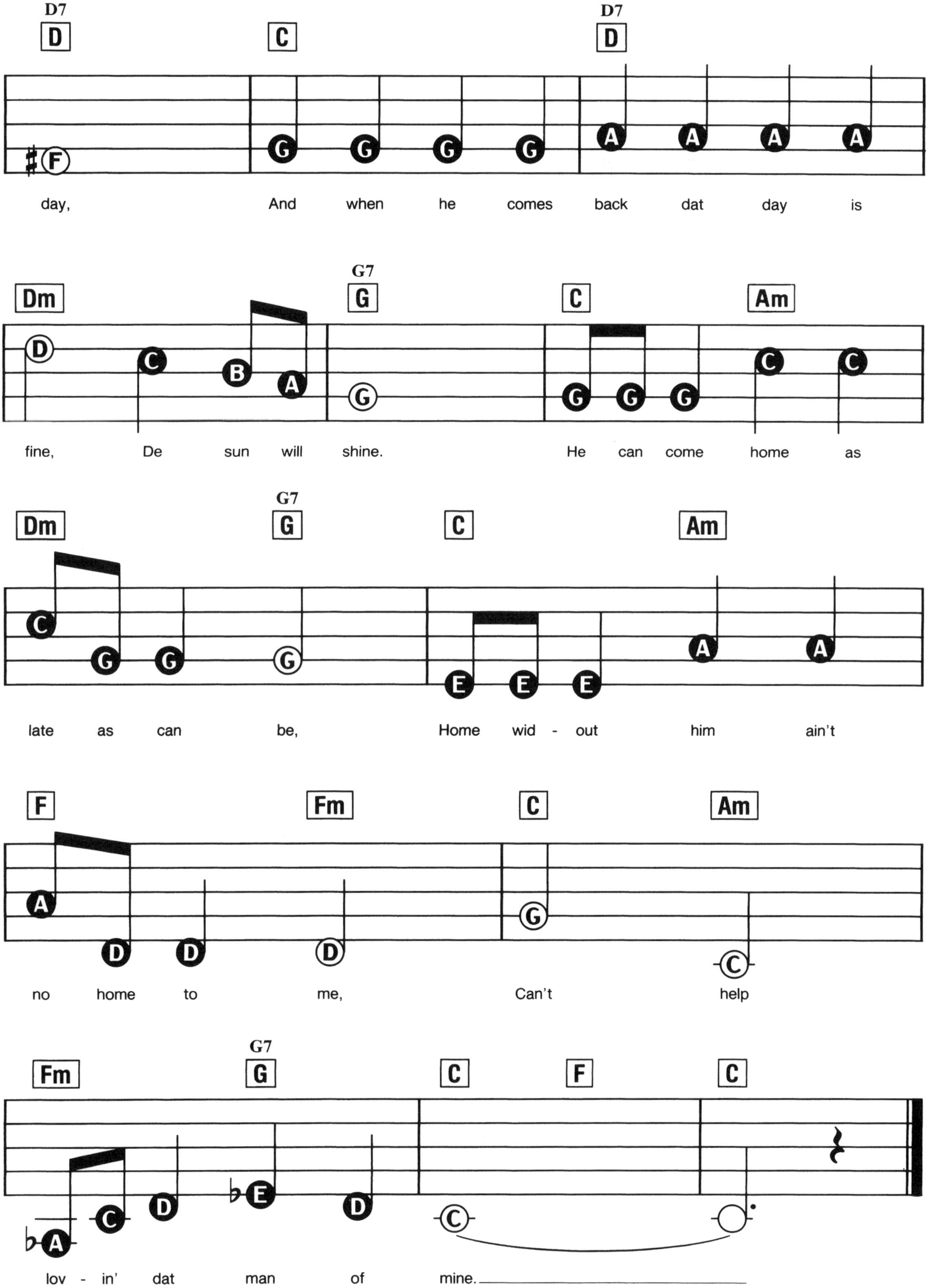
D7 C D7
day, And when he comes back dat day is
Dm G7 C Am
fine, De sun will shine. He can come home as
Dm G7 C Am
late as can be, Home wid - out him ain't
F Fm C Am
no home to me, Can't help
Fm G7 C F C
lov - in' dat man of mine.

Can't Take My Eyes Off of You

Registration 4
Rhythm: Medium Rock

Words and Music by Bob Crewe
and Bob Gaudio

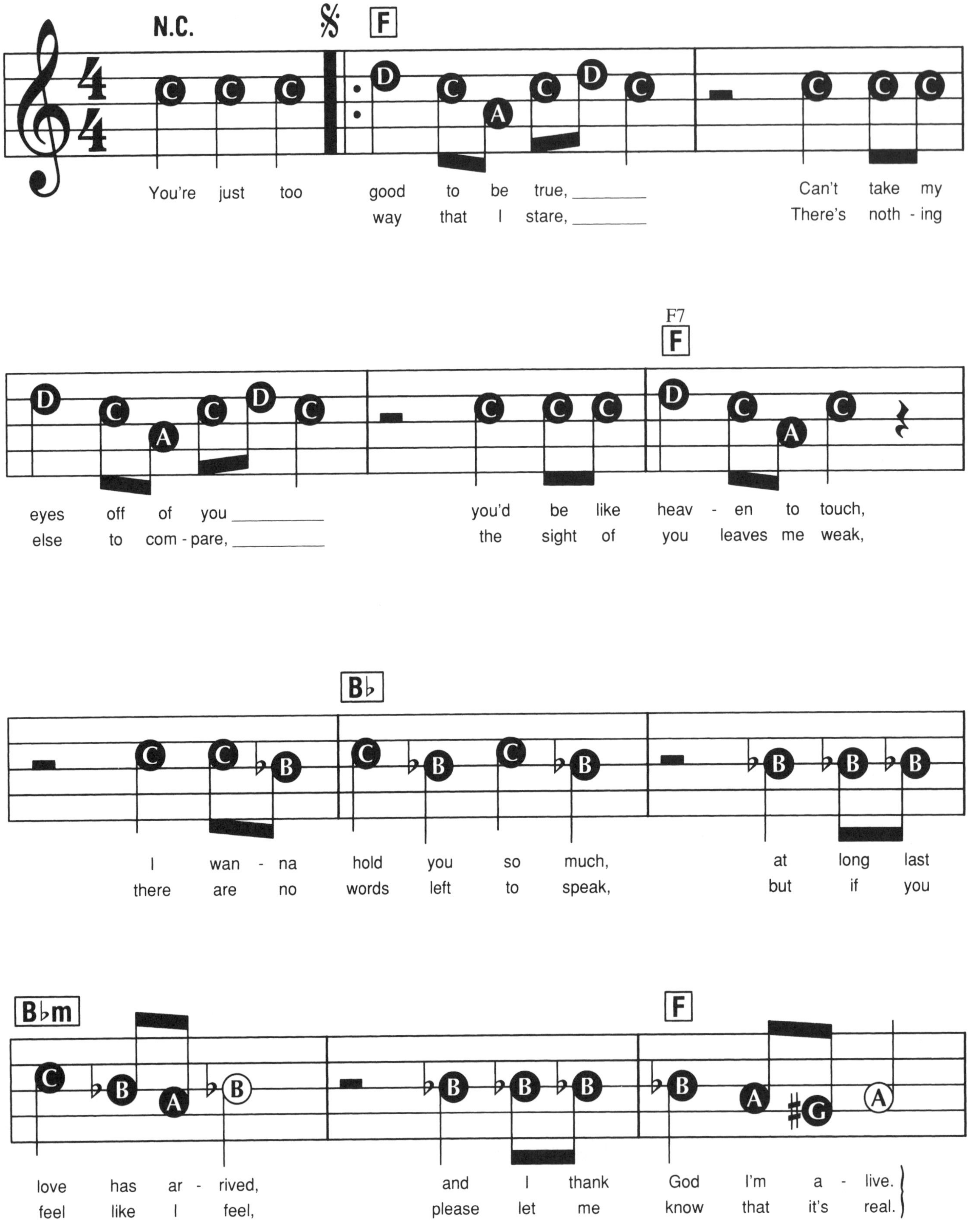
N.C.
F
You're just too good to be true,
way that I stare,
Can't take my
There's noth - ing
eyes off of you
else to com - pare,
F7
F
you'd be like heav - en to touch,
the sight of you leaves me weak,
B♭
I wan - na hold you so much,
there are no words left to speak,
at long last
but if you
B♭m
love has ar - rived,
feel like I feel,
F
and I thank God I'm a - live.
and please let me know that it's real.

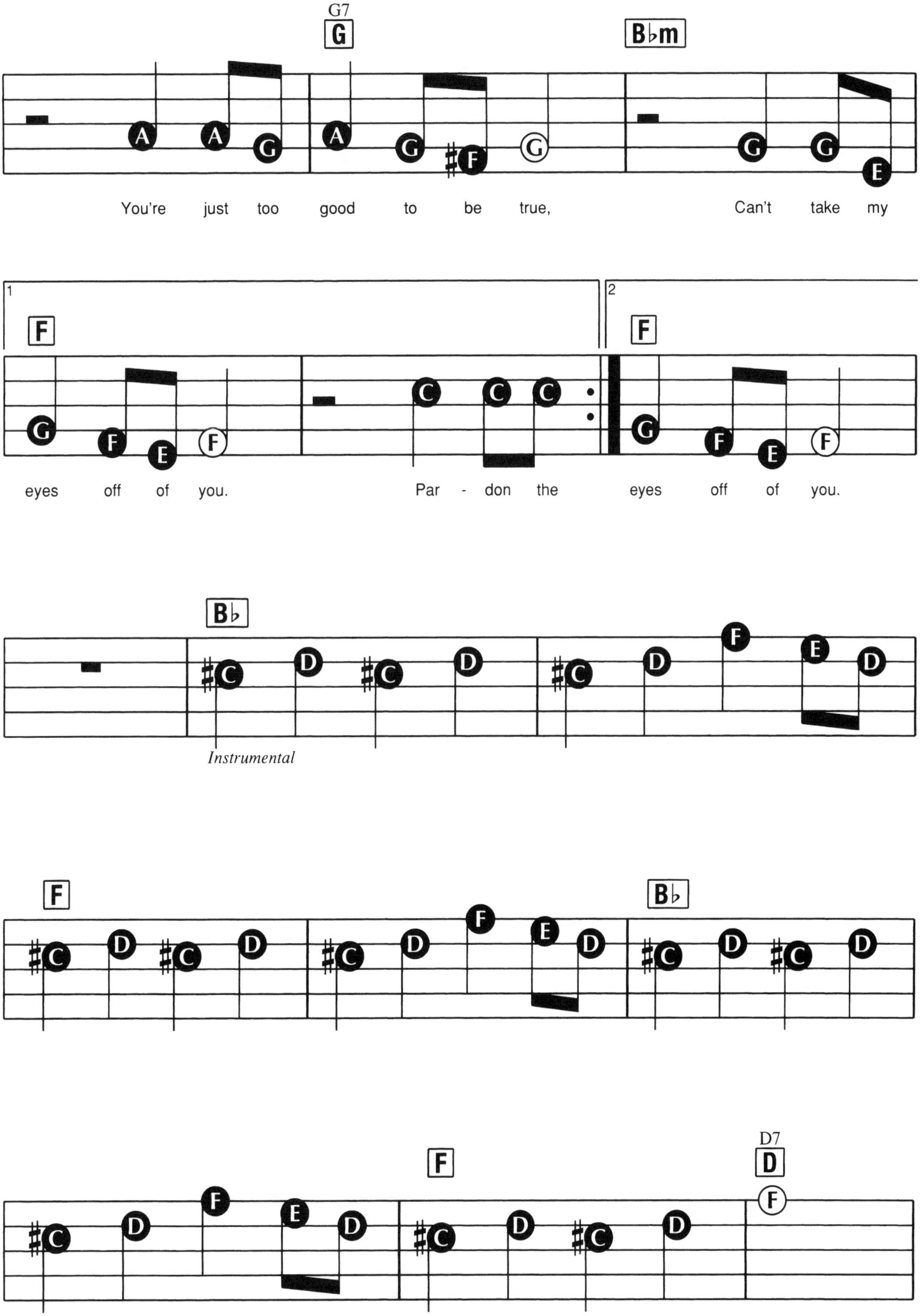
G7
G
B♭m
You're just too good to be true,
Can't take my
1
F
2
F
eyes off of you.
Par - don the
eyes off of you.
B♭
Instrumental
F
B♭
F
D7
D

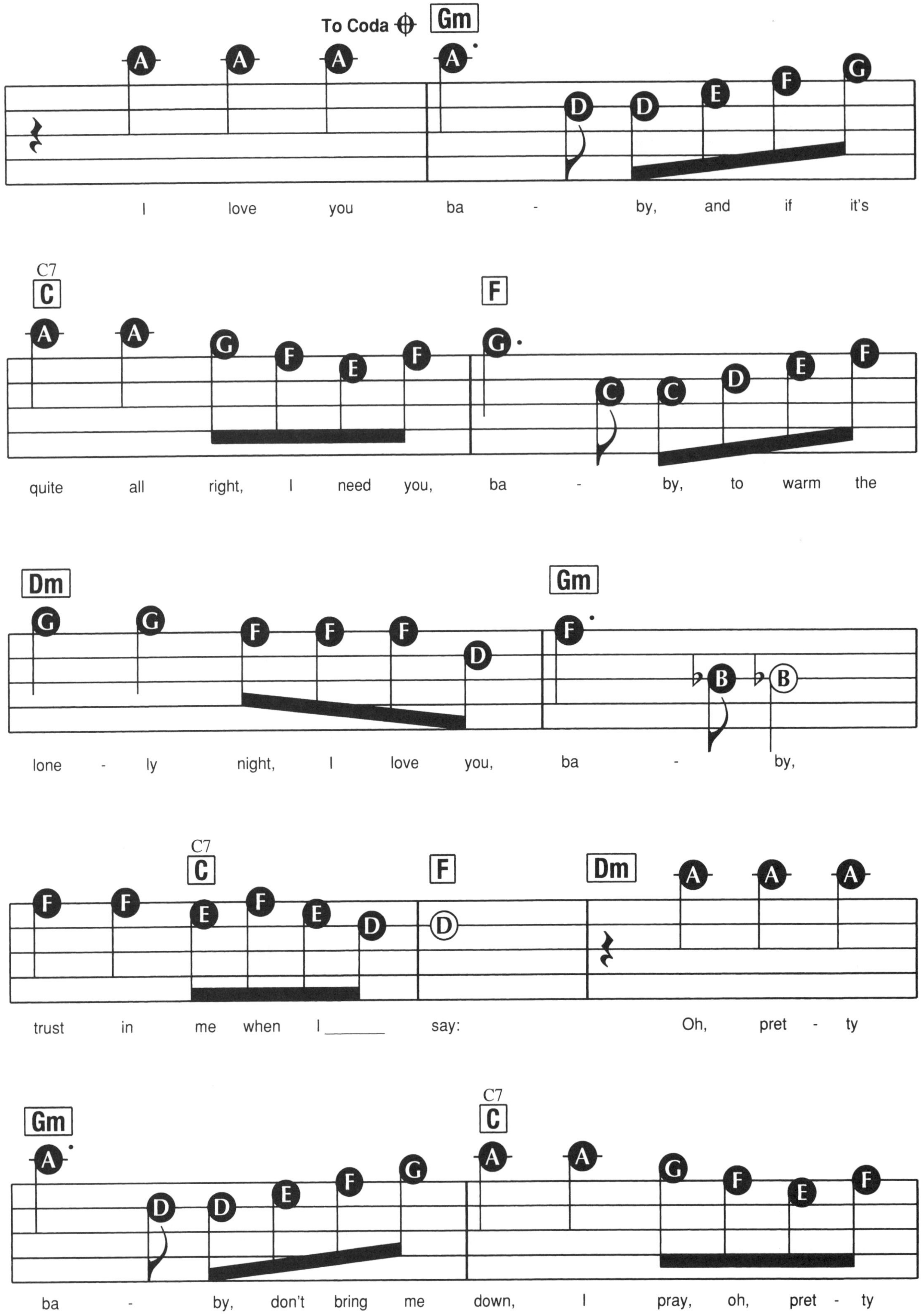
To Coda
Gm
I love you ba - by, and if it's
C7 C F
quite all right, I need you, ba - by, to warm the
Dm Gm
lone - ly night, I love you, ba - by,
C7 C F Dm
trust in me when I ______ say: Oh, pret - ty
Gm C7 C
ba - by, don't bring me down, I pray, oh, pret - ty

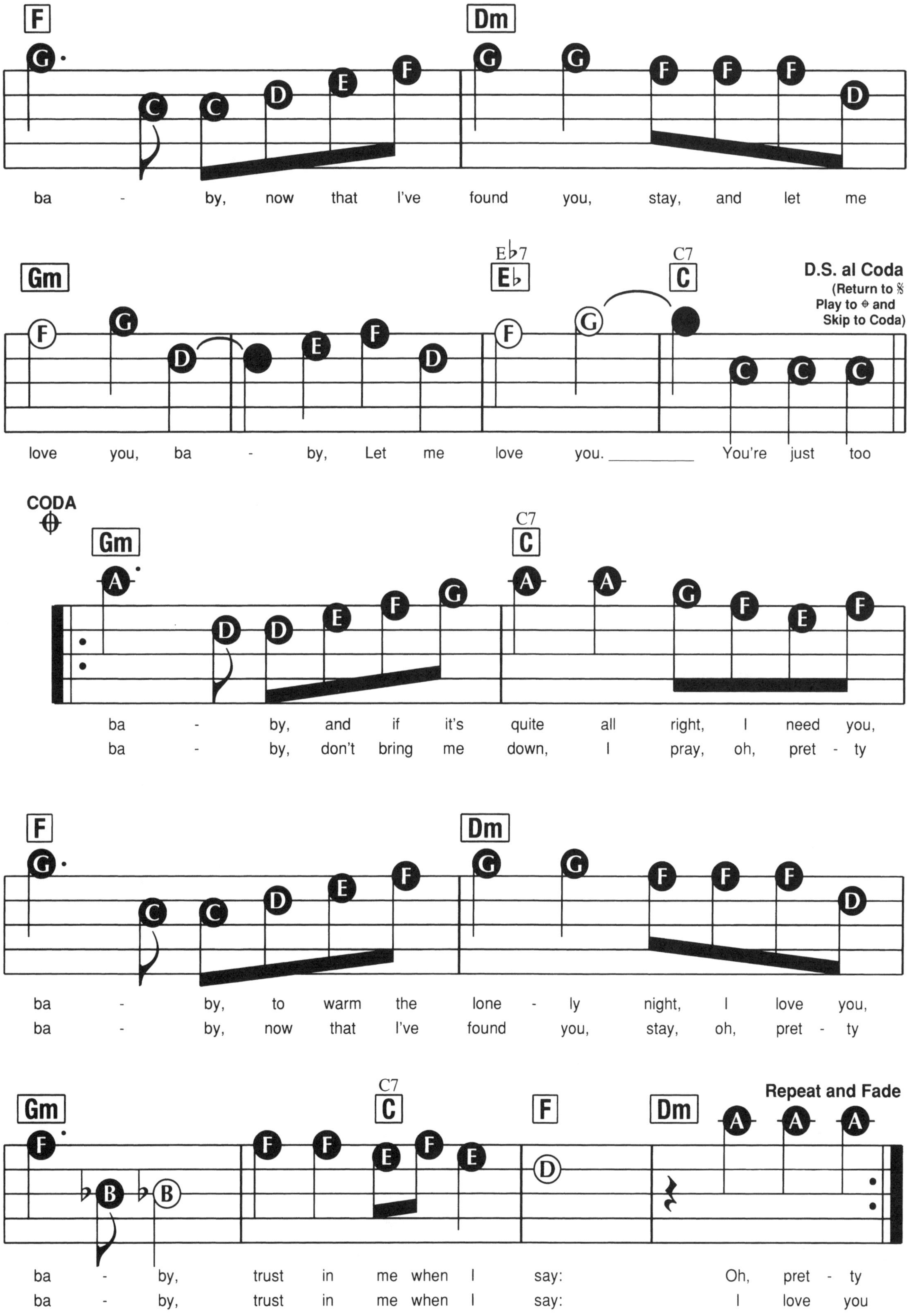
F Dm
ba - by, now that I've found you, stay, and let me
Gm E♭7 E♭ C7 C
D.S. al Coda
(Return to 𝄋 Play to ⊕ and Skip to Coda)
love you, ba - by, Let me love you. ___ You're just too
CODA
Gm C7 C
ba - by, and if it's quite all right, I need you,
ba - by, don't bring me down, I pray, oh, pret - ty
F Dm
ba - by, to warm the lone - ly night, I love you,
ba - by, now that I've found you, stay, oh, pret - ty
Gm C7 C F Dm
Repeat and Fade
ba - by, trust in me when I say: Oh, pret - ty
ba - by, trust in me when I say: I love you

Can't We Try

Registration 4
Rhythm: Medium Rock Ballad

Words and Music by Dan Hill
Additional Lyrics by Beverly Chapin-Hill

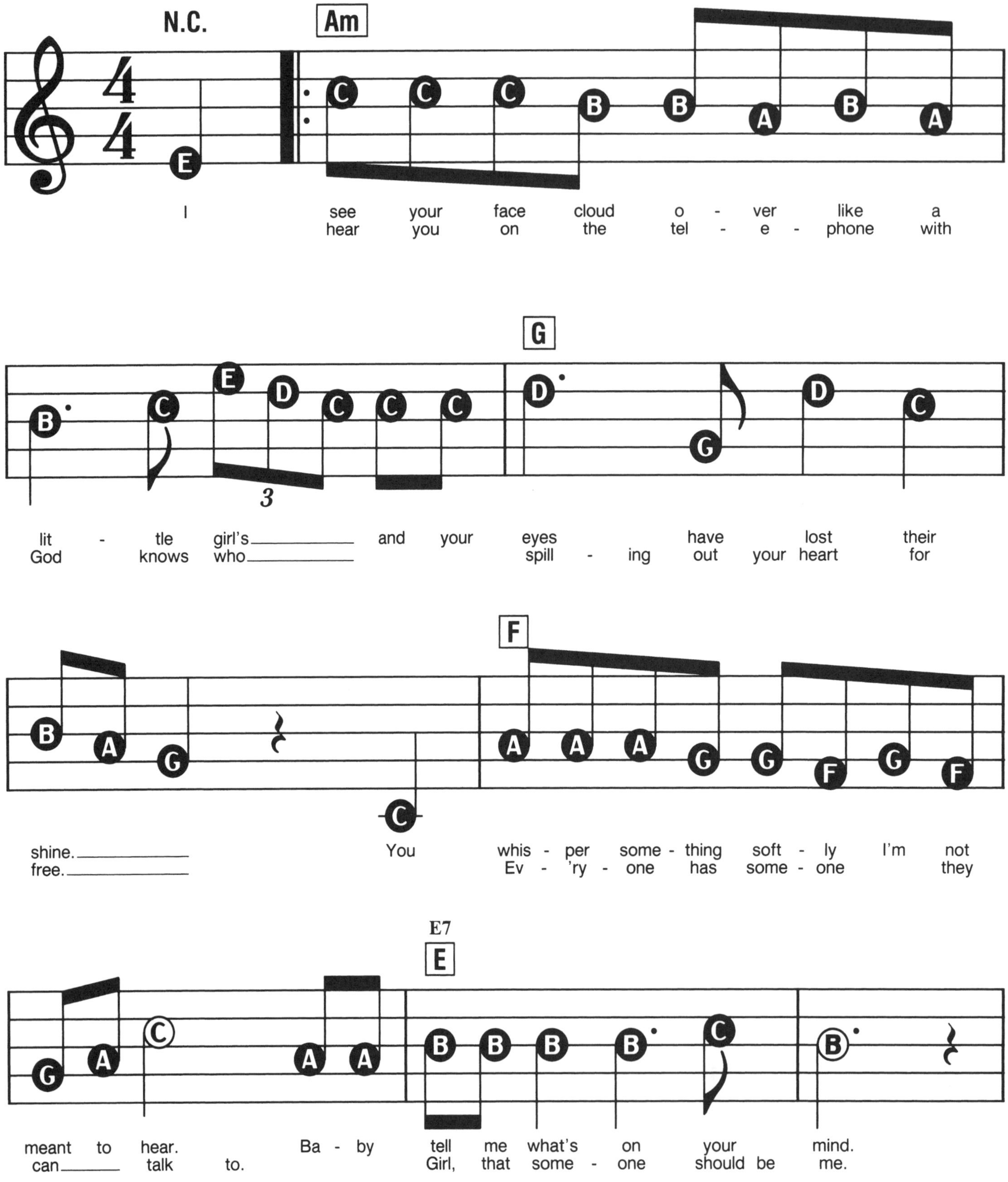
N.C.
Am
I see your face cloud o - ver like a
hear you on the tel - e - phone with
G
lit - tle girl's and your eyes have lost their
God knows who spill - ing out your heart for
F
shine. You whis - per some - thing soft - ly I'm not
free. Ev - 'ry - one has some - one they
E7
E
meant to hear. Ba - by tell me what's on your mind.
can talk to. Girl, that some - one should be me.

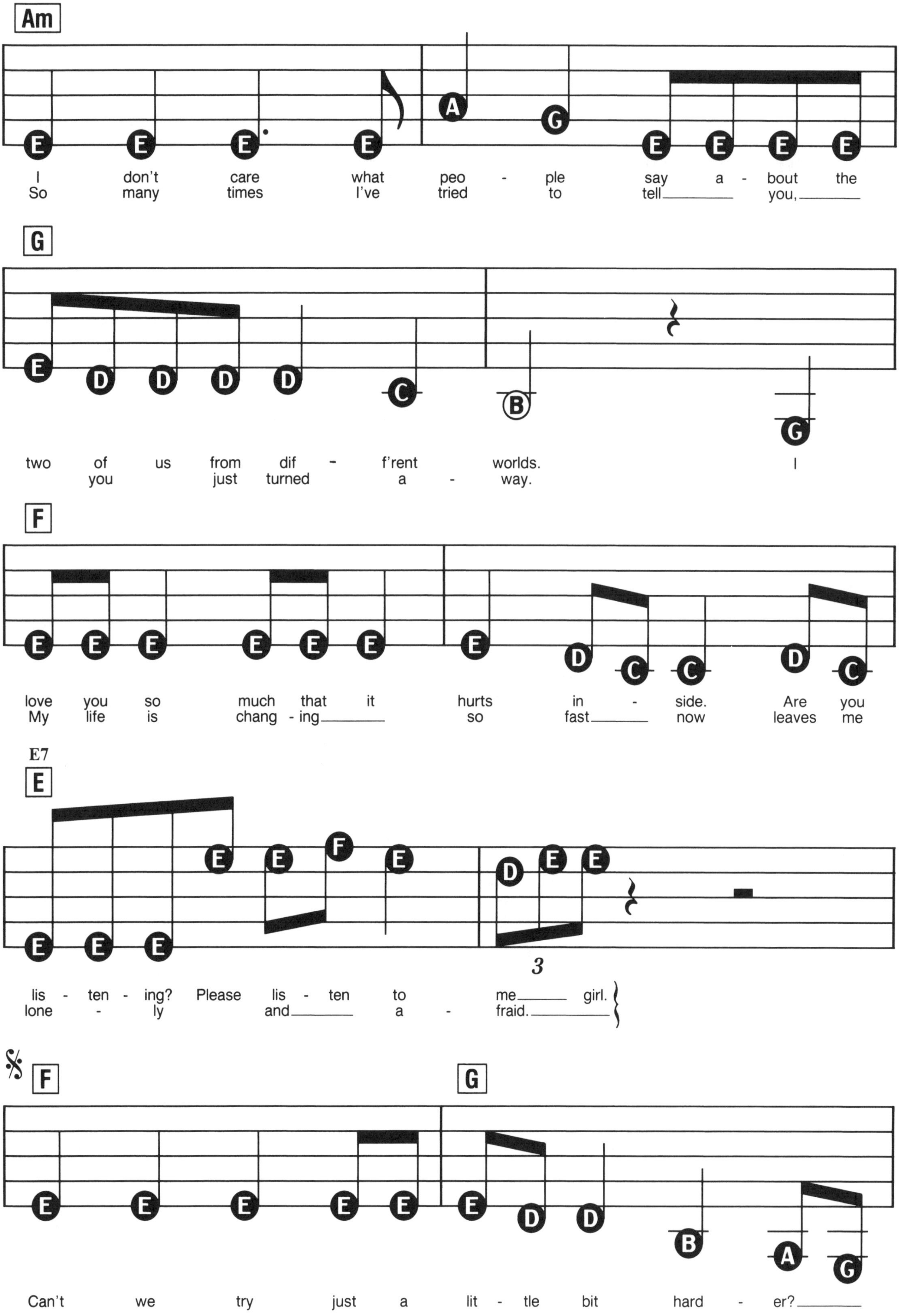
Am
I don't care what peo - ple say a - bout the
So many times I've tried to tell___ you,___
G
two of us from dif - f'rent worlds. I
you just turned a - way.
F
love you so much that it hurts in - side. Are you
My life is chang - ing___ so fast___ now leaves me
E7
E
lis - ten - ing? Please lis - ten to me___ girl.
lone - ly and___ a - fraid.___
3
F
G
Can't we try just a lit - tle bit hard - er?___

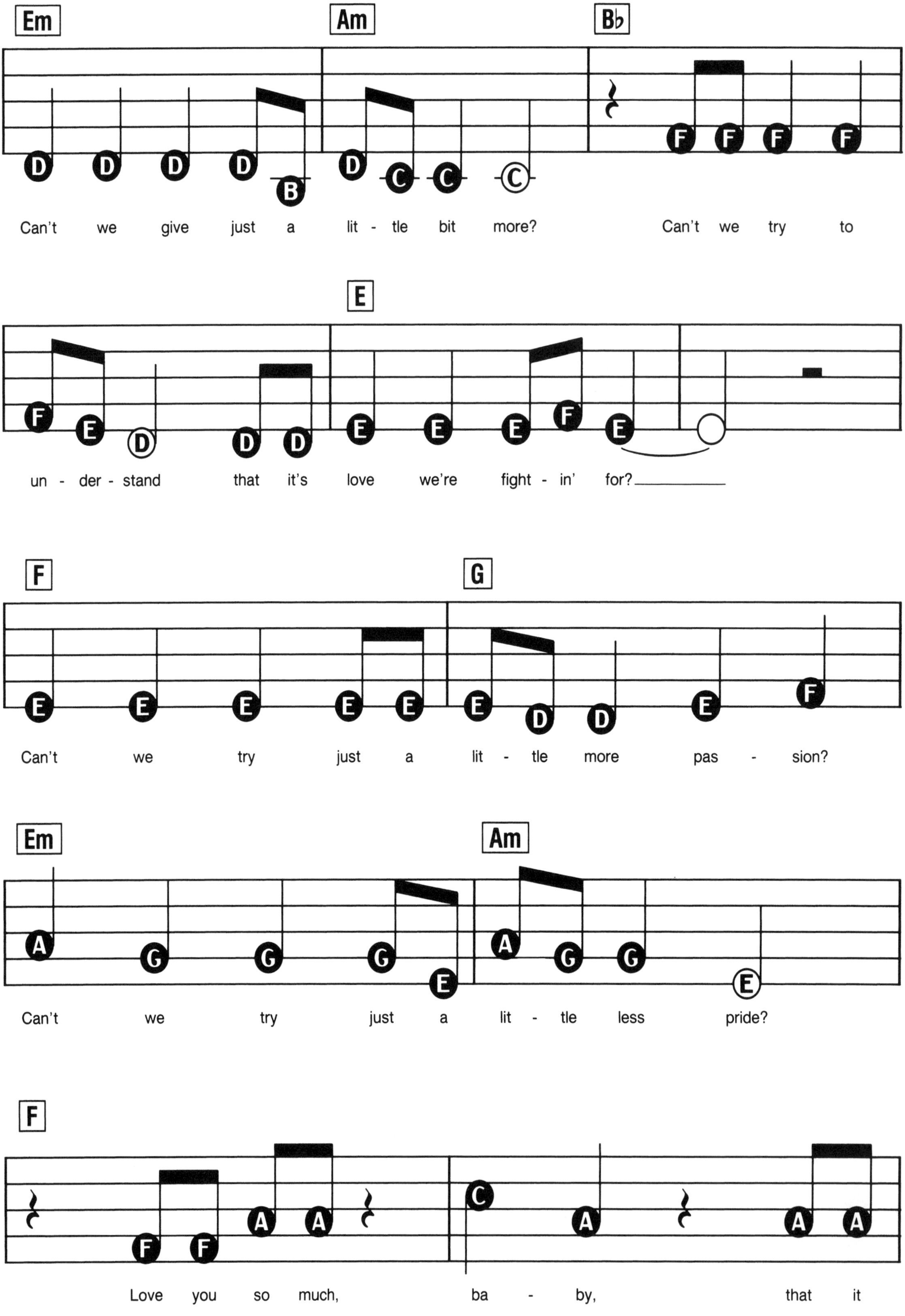
Em Am B♭
Can't we give just a lit - tle bit more? Can't we try to
E
un - der - stand that it's love we're fight - in' for?
F G
Can't we try just a lit - tle more pas - sion?
Em Am
Can't we try just a lit - tle less pride?
F
Love you so much, ba - by, that it

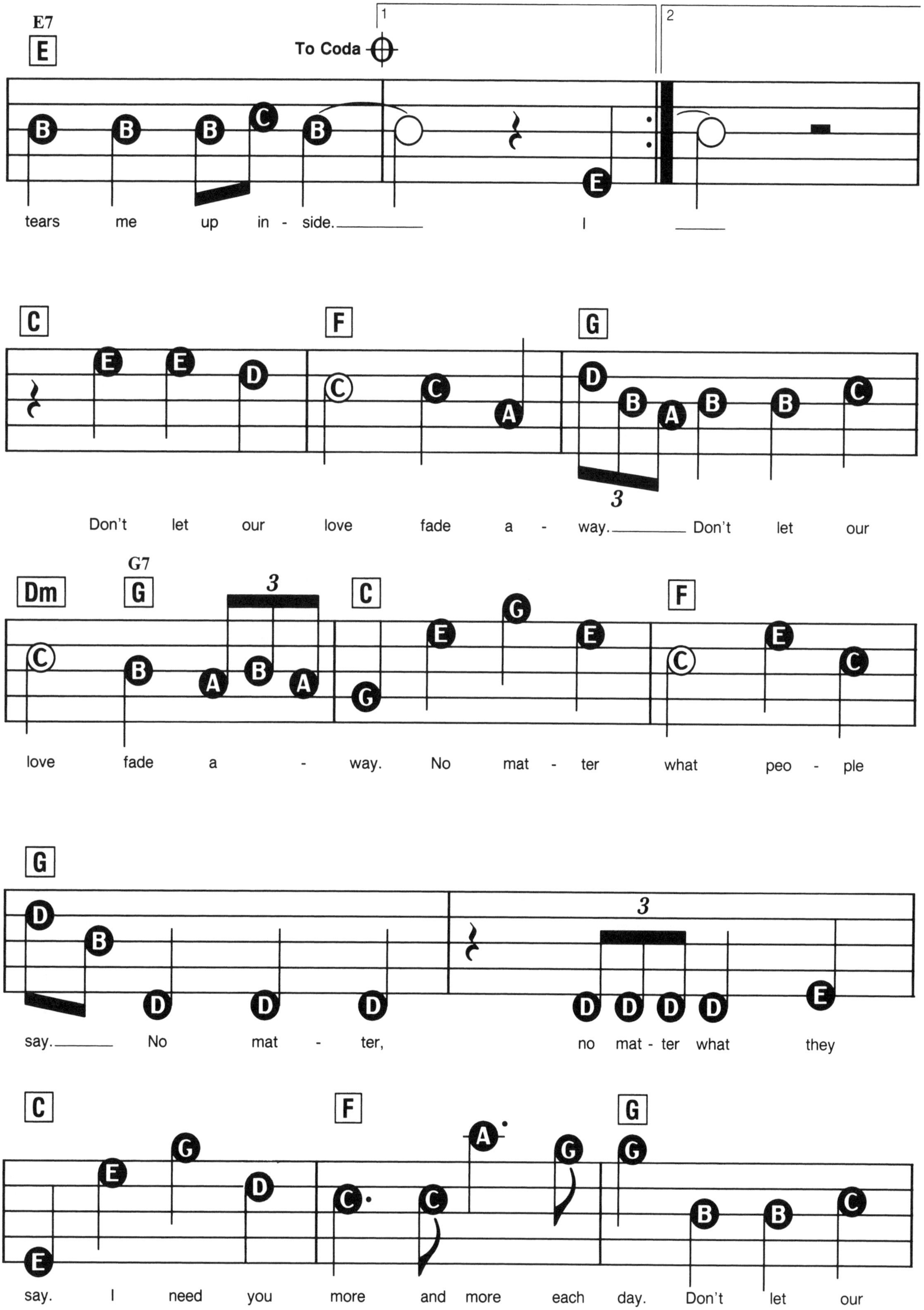
E7
E
To Coda
1
2
tears me up in - side. I
C
F
G
Don't let our love fade a - way. Don't let our
Dm
G7
G
C
F
love fade a - way. No mat - ter what peo - ple
G
say. No mat - ter, no mat - ter what they
C
F
G
say. I need you more and more each day. Don't let our

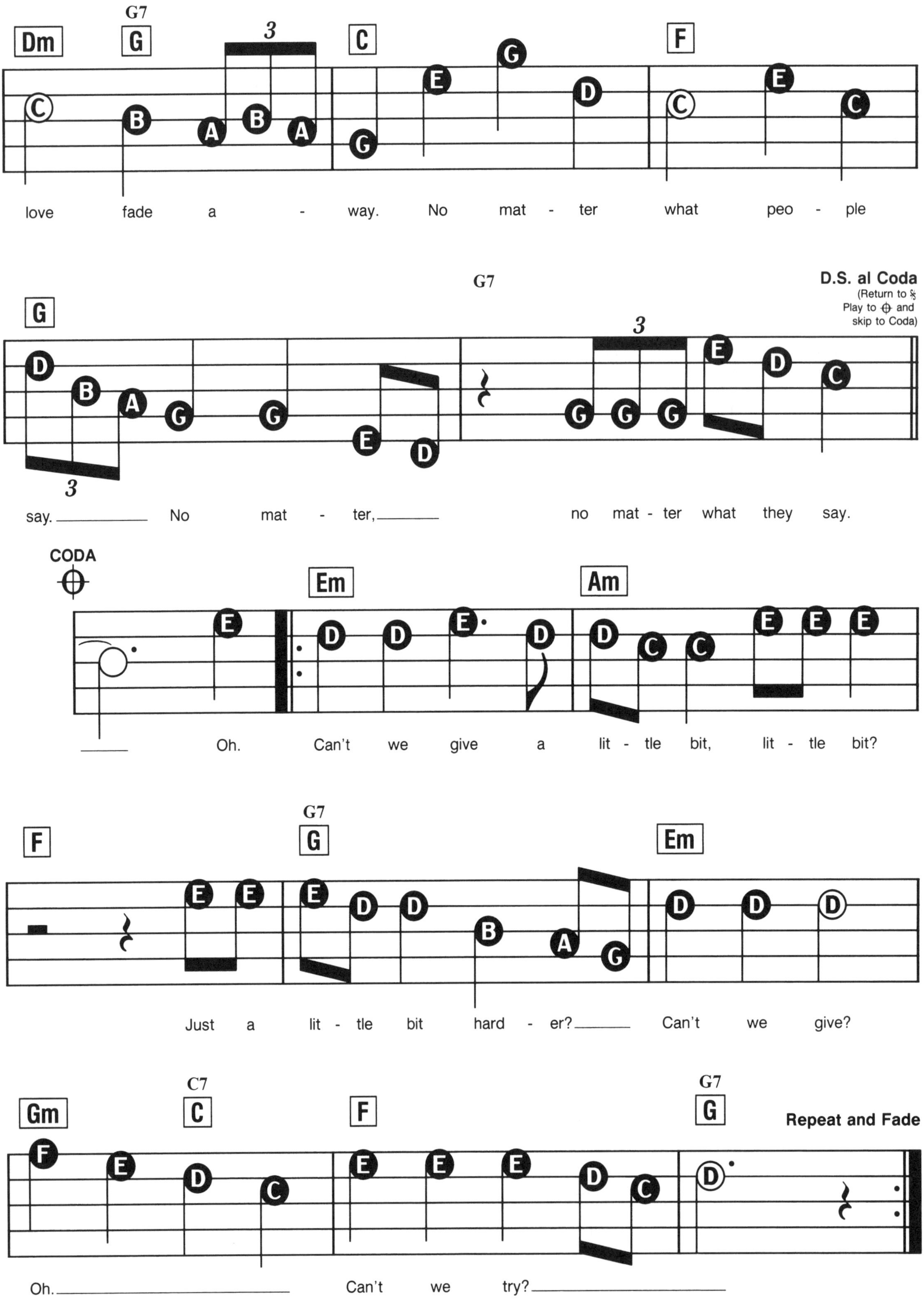

Dm G7 G C F
love fade a - way. No mat - ter what peo - ple
G G7
D.S. al Coda
(Return to 𝄋 Play to ⊕ and skip to Coda)
say. No mat - ter, no mat - ter what they say.
CODA
Em Am
Oh. Can't we give a lit - tle bit, lit - tle bit?
F G7 G Em
Just a lit - tle bit hard - er? Can't we give?
Gm C7 C F G7 G
Repeat and Fade
Oh. Can't we try?

The Colour of Love

Registration 5
Rhythm: Rock

Words and Music by Jolyon Skinner,
Barry Eastmond, Wayne Brathwaite and Billy Ocean

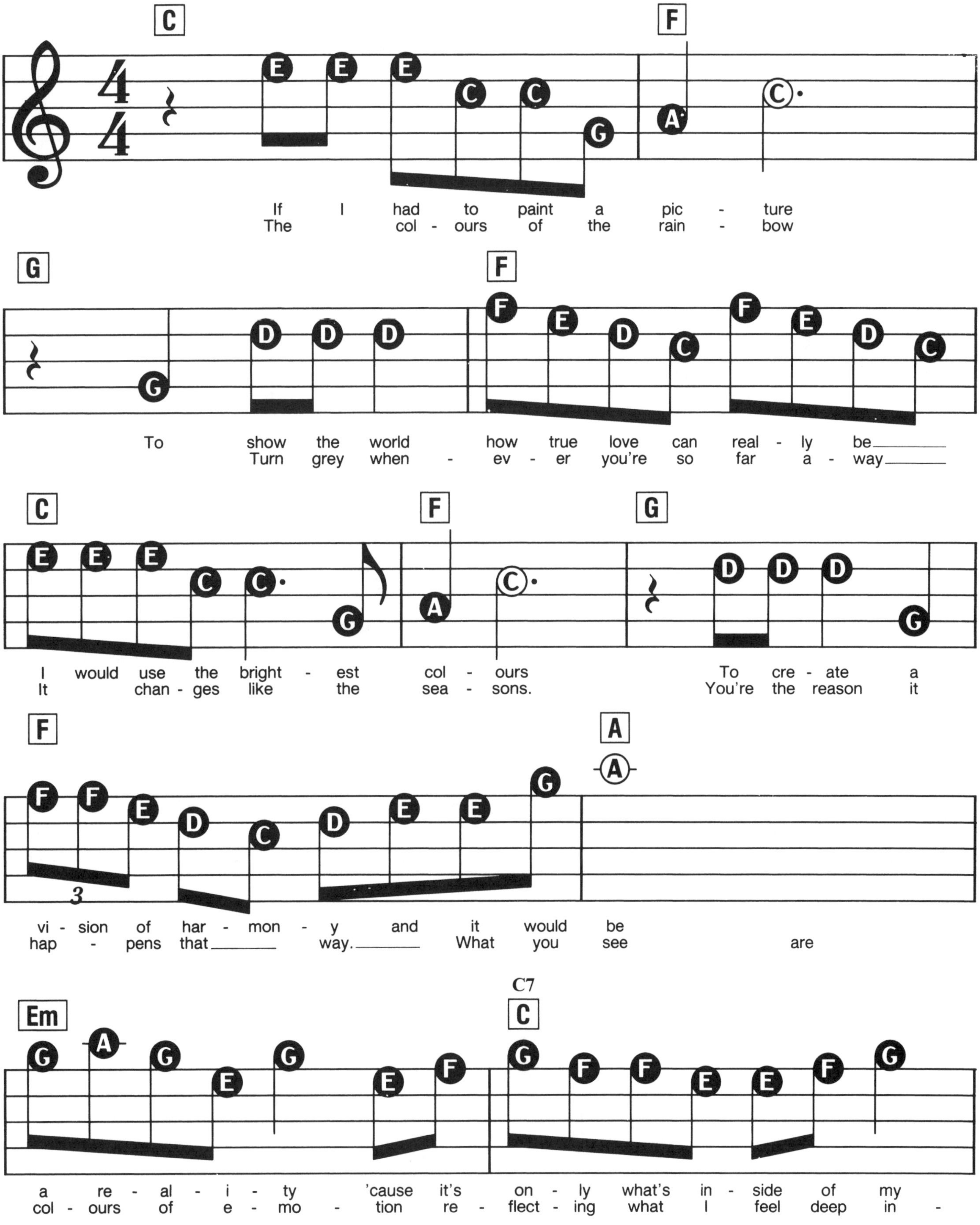
If I had to paint a pic - ture
The col - ours of the rain - bow
To show the world how true love can real - ly be
Turn grey when - ev - er you're so far a - way
I would use the bright - est col - ours To cre - ate a
It chan - ges like the sea - sons. You're the reason it
vi - sion of har - mon - y and it would be
hap - pens that way. What you see are
a re - al - i - ty 'cause it's on - ly what's in - side of my
col - ours of e - mo - tion re - flect - ing what I feel deep in -
C7

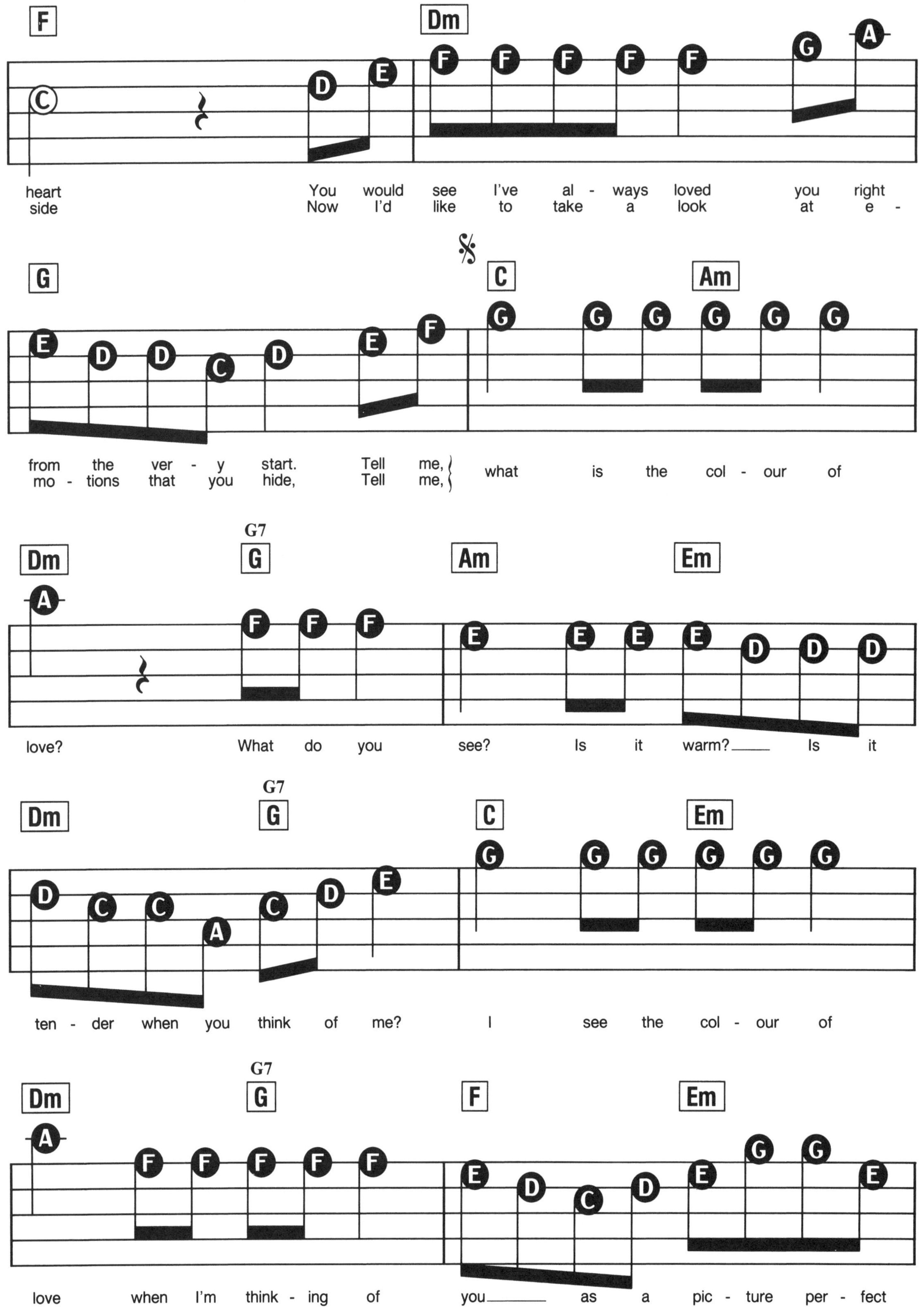
F Dm
heart You would see I've al - ways loved you right
side Now I'd like to take a look at e -
G C Am
from the ver - y start. Tell me, what is the col - our of
mo - tions that you hide, Tell me,
Dm G7 G Am Em
love? What do you see? Is it warm? Is it
Dm G7 G C Em
ten - der when you think of me? I see the col - our of
Dm G7 G F Em
love when I'm think - ing of you as a pic - ture per - fect

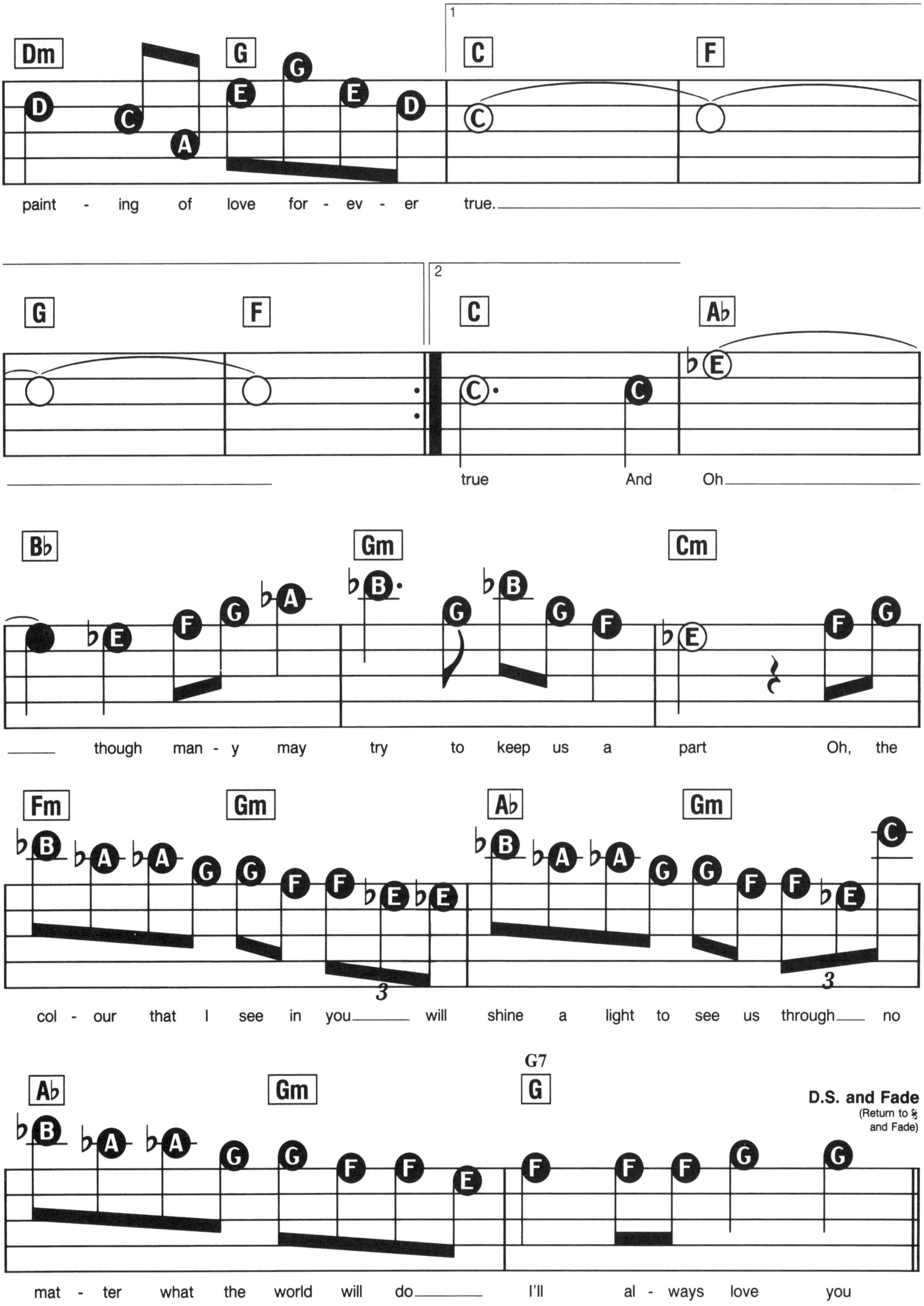
Dm G C F
painting of love forever true.
G F C Ab
true And Oh
Bb Gm Cm
though many may try to keep us apart Oh, the
Fm Gm Ab Gm
colour that I see in you will shine a light to see us through no
Ab Gm G7 G
matter what the world will do I'll always love you
D.S. and Fade
(Return to 𝄋 and Fade)

Canadian Sunset

Registration 2
Rhythm: Fox Trot or Swing

Words by Norman Gimbel
Music by Eddie Heywood

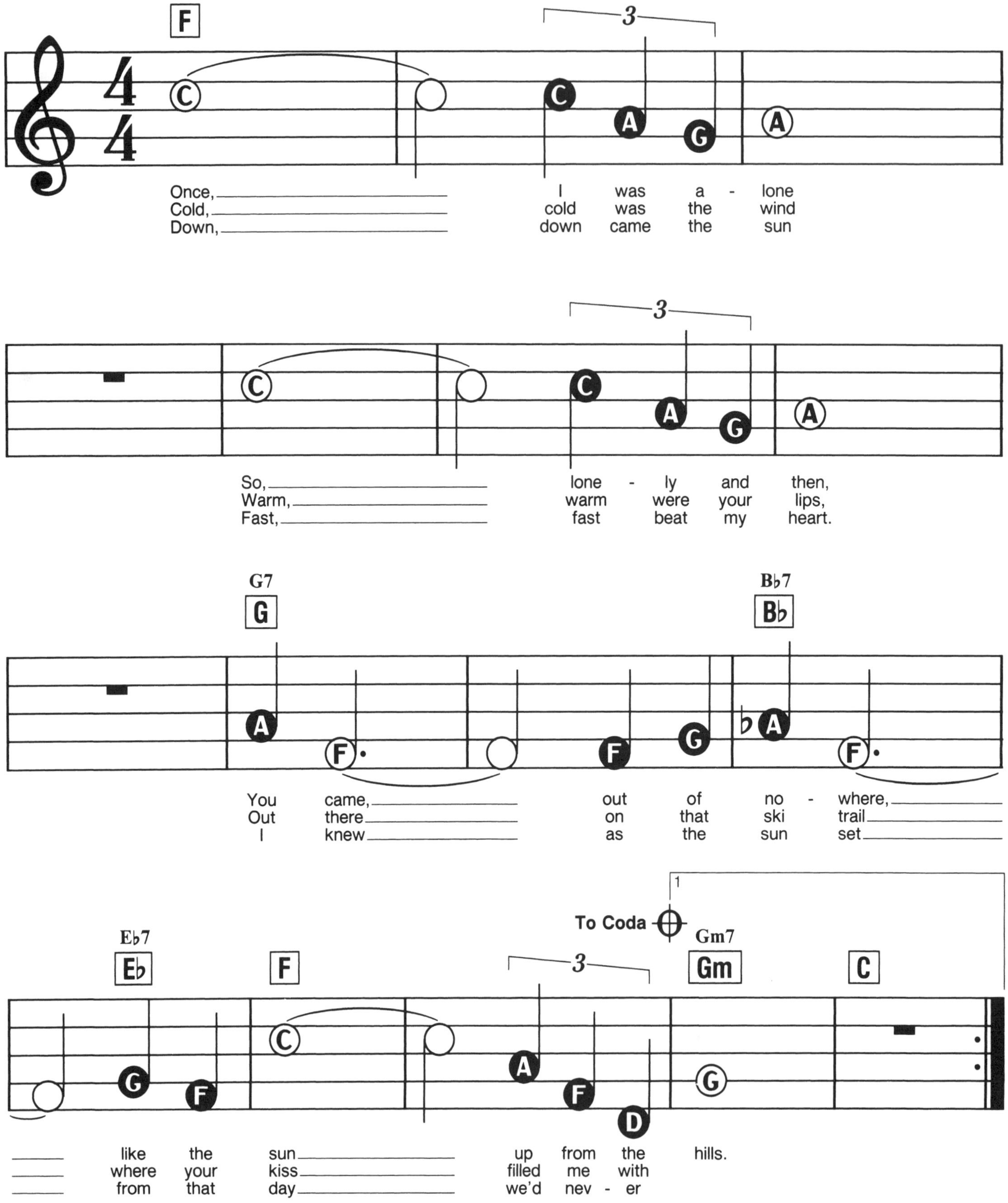
F
3
Once, I was a - lone
Cold, cold was the wind
Down, down came the sun
3
So, lone - ly and then,
Warm, warm were your lips,
Fast, fast beat my heart.
G7
G
Bb7
Bb
You came, out of no - where,
Out there on that ski trail
I knew as the sun set
Eb7
Eb
F
To Coda
3
Gm7
Gm
C
1
like the sun up from the hills.
where your kiss filled me with
from that day we'd nev - er

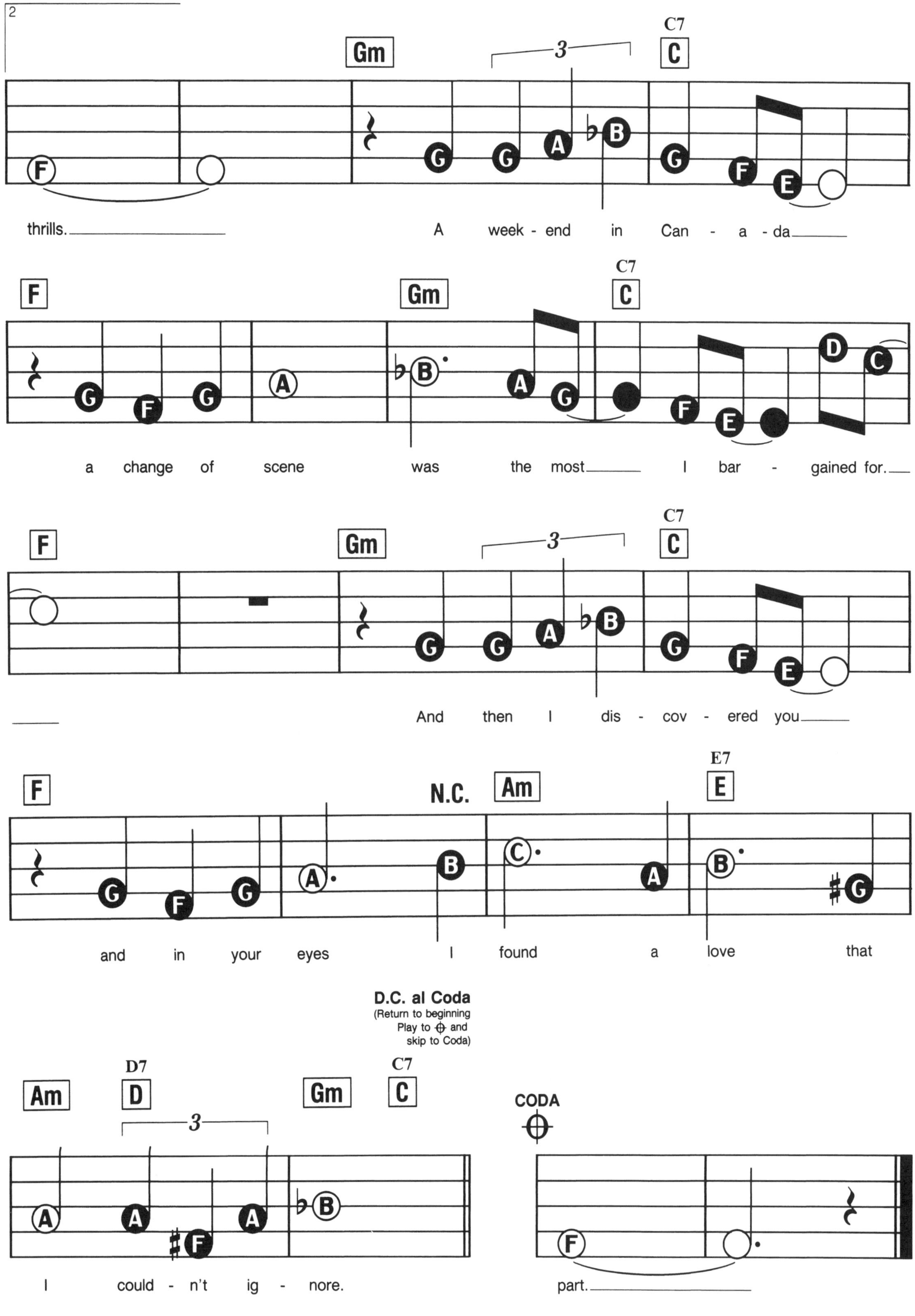
2
Gm
C7 C
thrills. A week - end in Can - a - da
F Gm C7 C
a change of scene was the most I bar - gained for.
F Gm C7 C
And then I dis - cov - ered you
F N.C. Am E7 E
and in your eyes I found a love that
D.C. al Coda
(Return to beginning
Play to ⊕ and
skip to Coda)
Am D7 D Gm C7 C
CODA
I could - n't ig - nore.
part.

Chanson D'Amour
(The Ra-Da-Da-Da-Da Song)

Registration 7
Rhythm: Swing or Jazz

Words and Music by
Wayne Shanklin

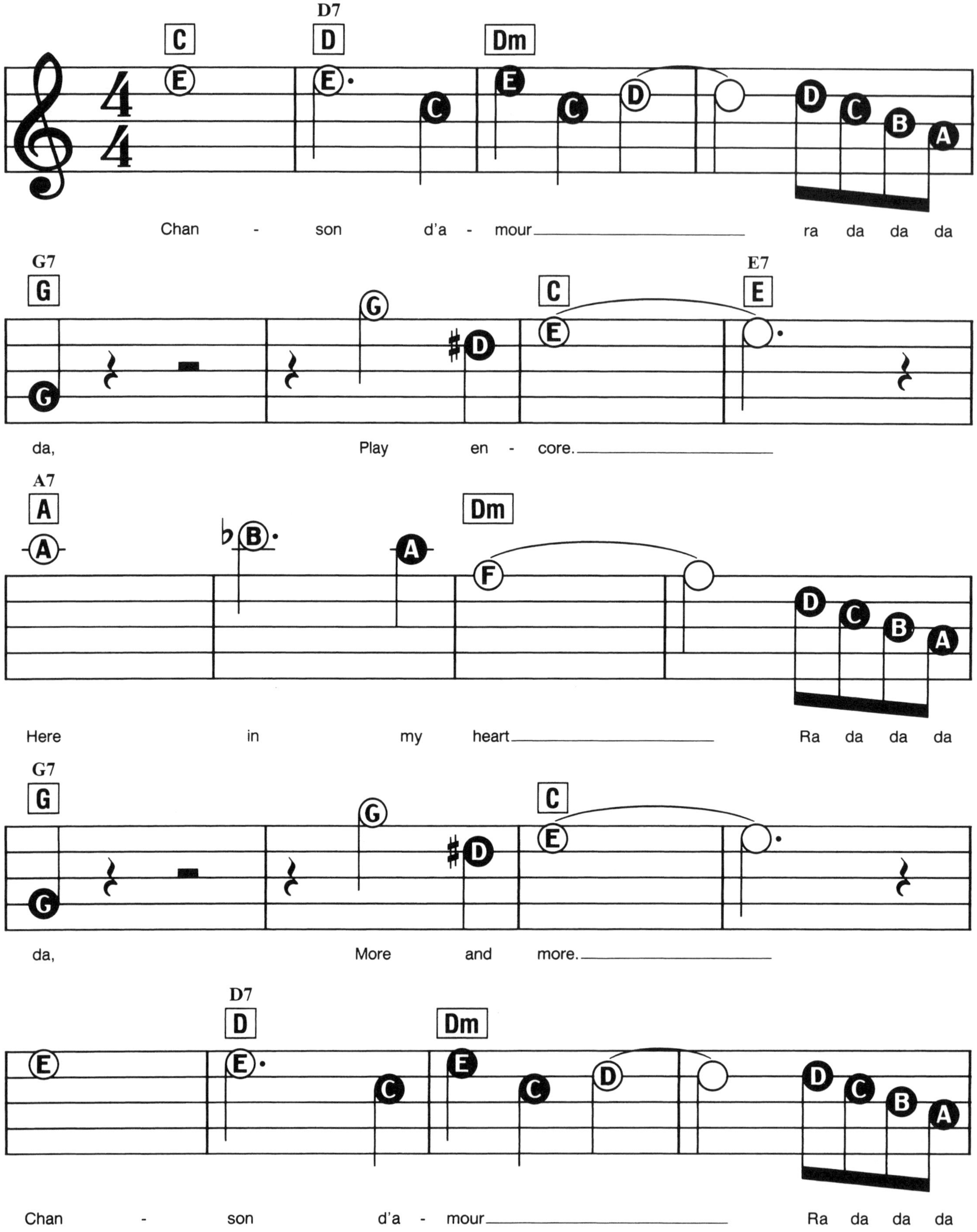
D7 G7 E7 A7
C D Dm G C E A Dm G C D Dm
Chan - son d'a - mour ra da da da
da, Play en - core.
Here in my heart Ra da da da
da, More and more.
Chan - son d'a - mour Ra da da da

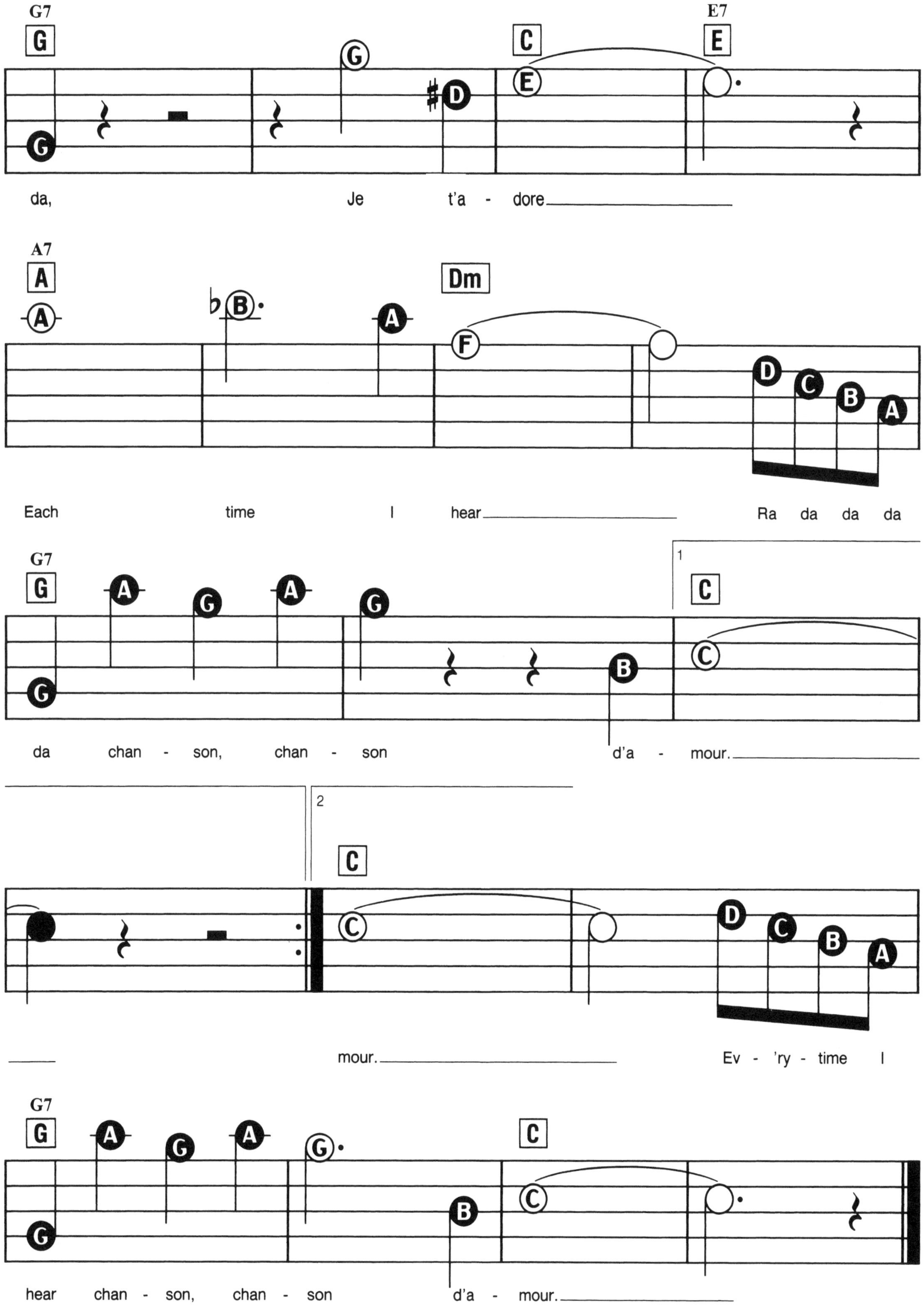
G7 G
C
E7 E
da, Je t'a - dore
A7 A
Dm
Each time I hear Ra da da da
G7 G
1
C
da chan - son, chan - son d'a - mour.
2
C
mour. Ev - 'ry - time I
G7 G
C
hear chan - son, chan - son d'a - mour.

Eternal Flame

Registration 4
Rhythm: Rock or 8-Beat

Words and Music by Billy Steinberg,
Tom Kelly and Susanna Hoffs

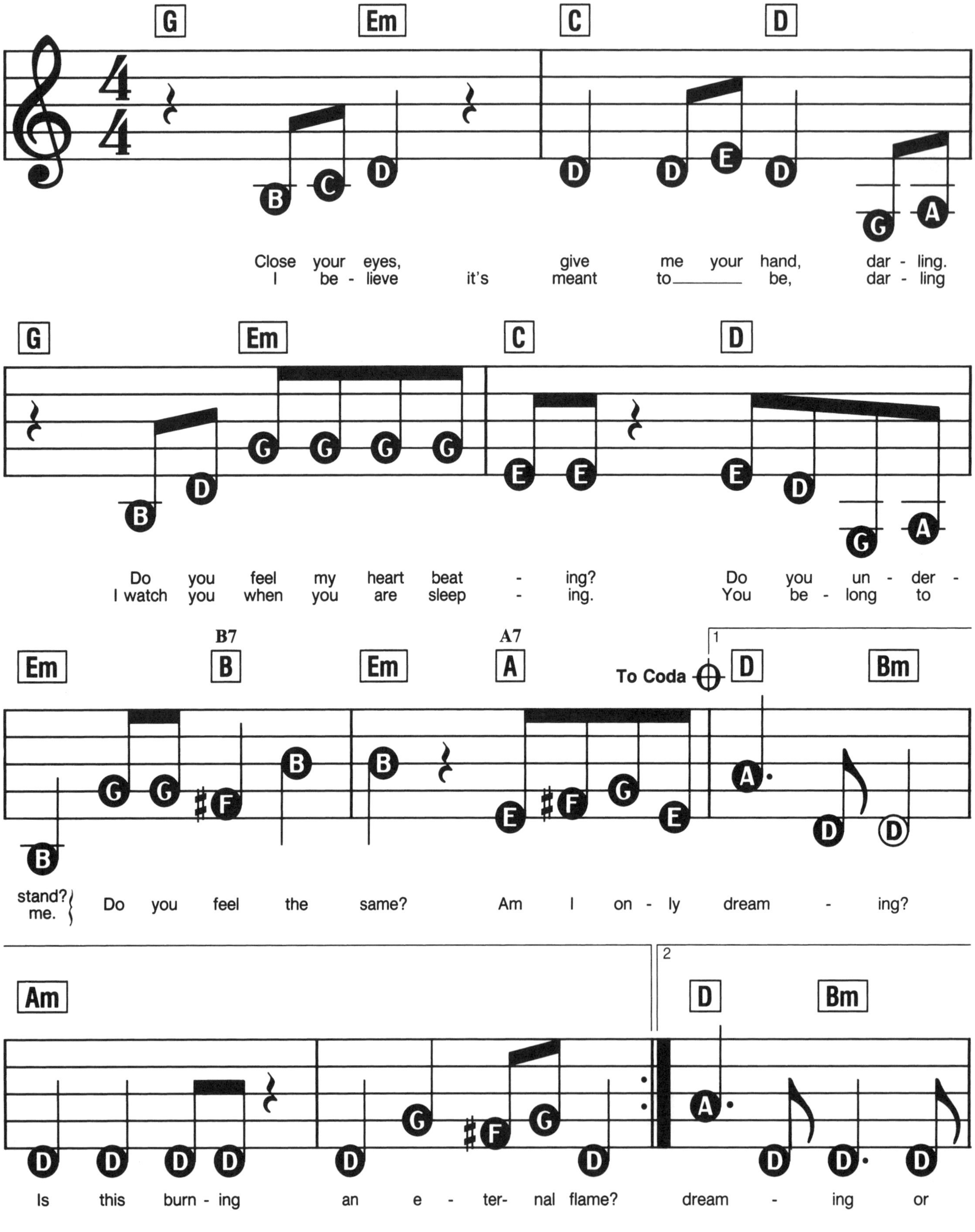
G Em C D
Close your eyes, give me your hand, dar - ling.
I be - lieve it's meant to be, dar - ling
G Em C D
Do you feel my heart beat - ing? Do you un - der -
I watch you when you are sleep - ing. You be - long to
Em B7 B Em A7 A To Coda 1 D Bm
stand? me. Do you feel the same? Am I on - ly dream - ing?
Am 2 D Bm
Is this burn - ing an e - ter- nal flame? dream - ing or

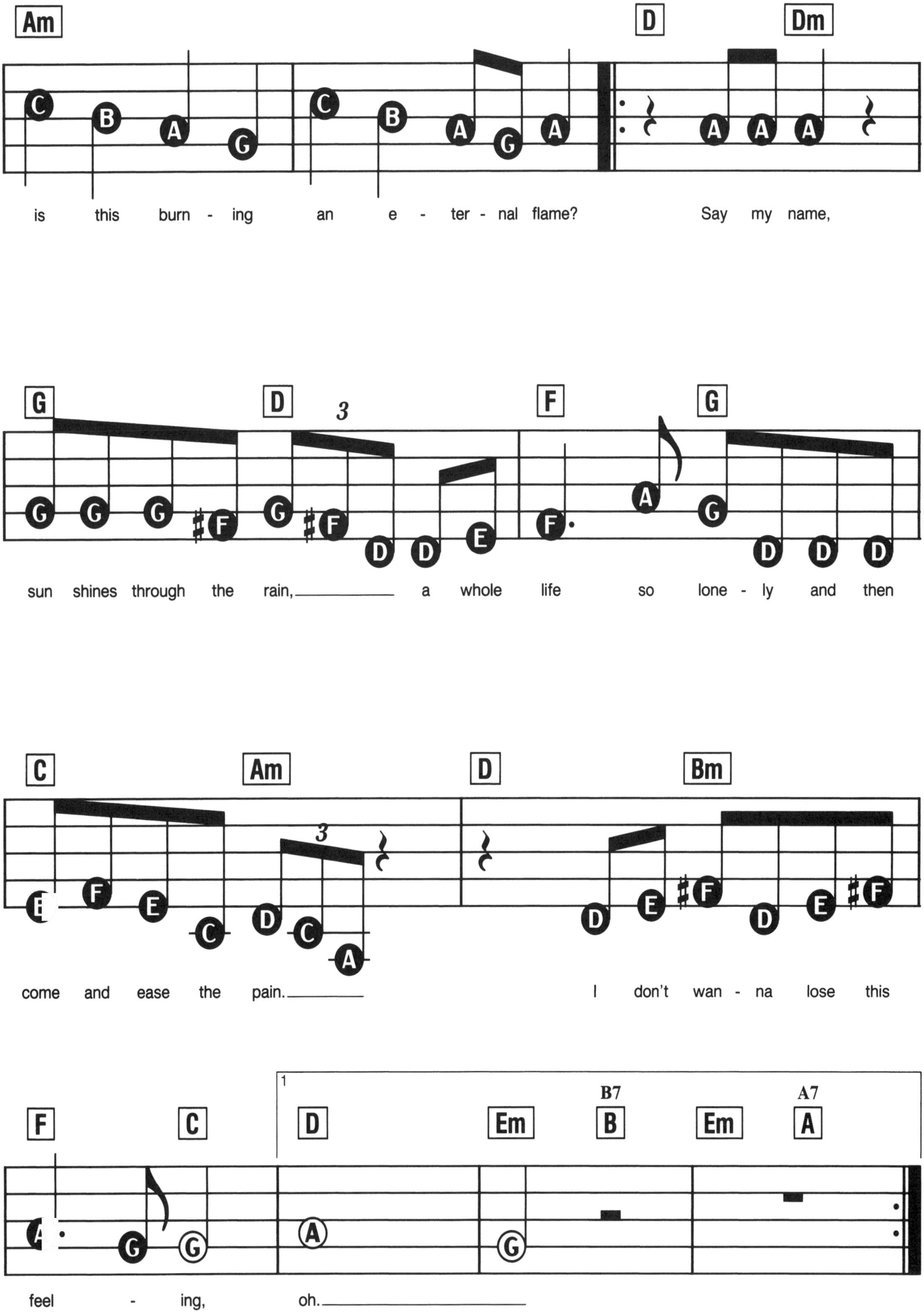
Am
D
Dm
is this burn - ing an e - ter - nal flame?
Say my name,
G
D
3
F
G
sun shines through the rain, a whole life so lone - ly and then
C
Am
3
D
Bm
come and ease the pain.
I don't wan - na lose this
F
C
1
D
Em
B7
B
Em
A7
A
feel - ing,
oh.

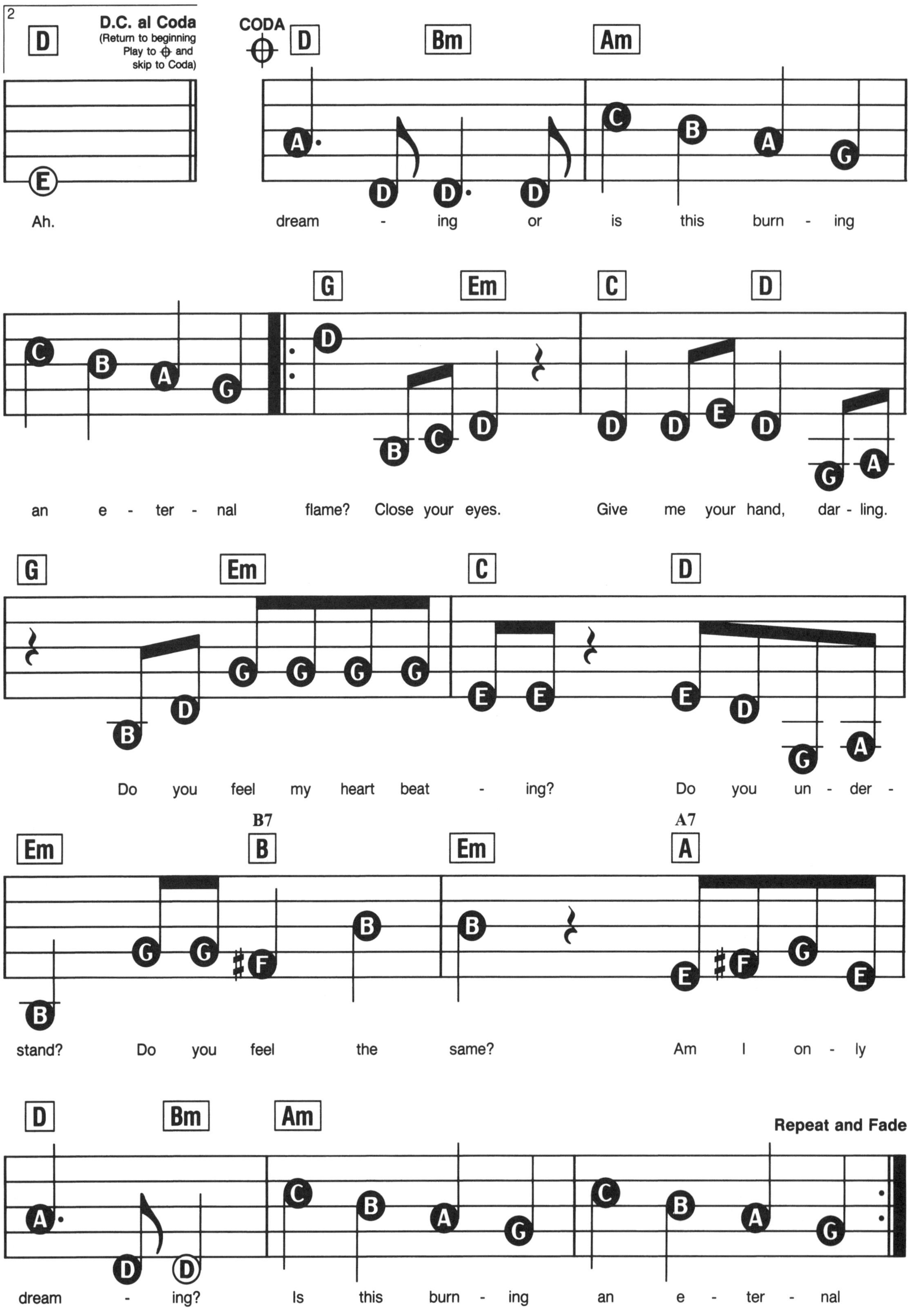
2
D
D.C. al Coda
(Return to beginning
Play to ⊕ and
skip to Coda)
Ah.
CODA
D Bm Am
dream - ing or is this burn - ing
an e - ter - nal
G Em C D
flame? Close your eyes. Give me your hand, dar - ling.
G Em C D
Do you feel my heart beat - ing? Do you un - der -
Em B7 B Em A7 A
stand? Do you feel the same? Am I on - ly
D Bm Am
Repeat and Fade
dream - ing? Is this burn - ing an e - ter - nal

For the First Time

from ONE FINE DAY

Registration 8
Rhythm: Ballad or Pop

Words and Music by James Newton Howard, Jud Friedman and Allan Rich

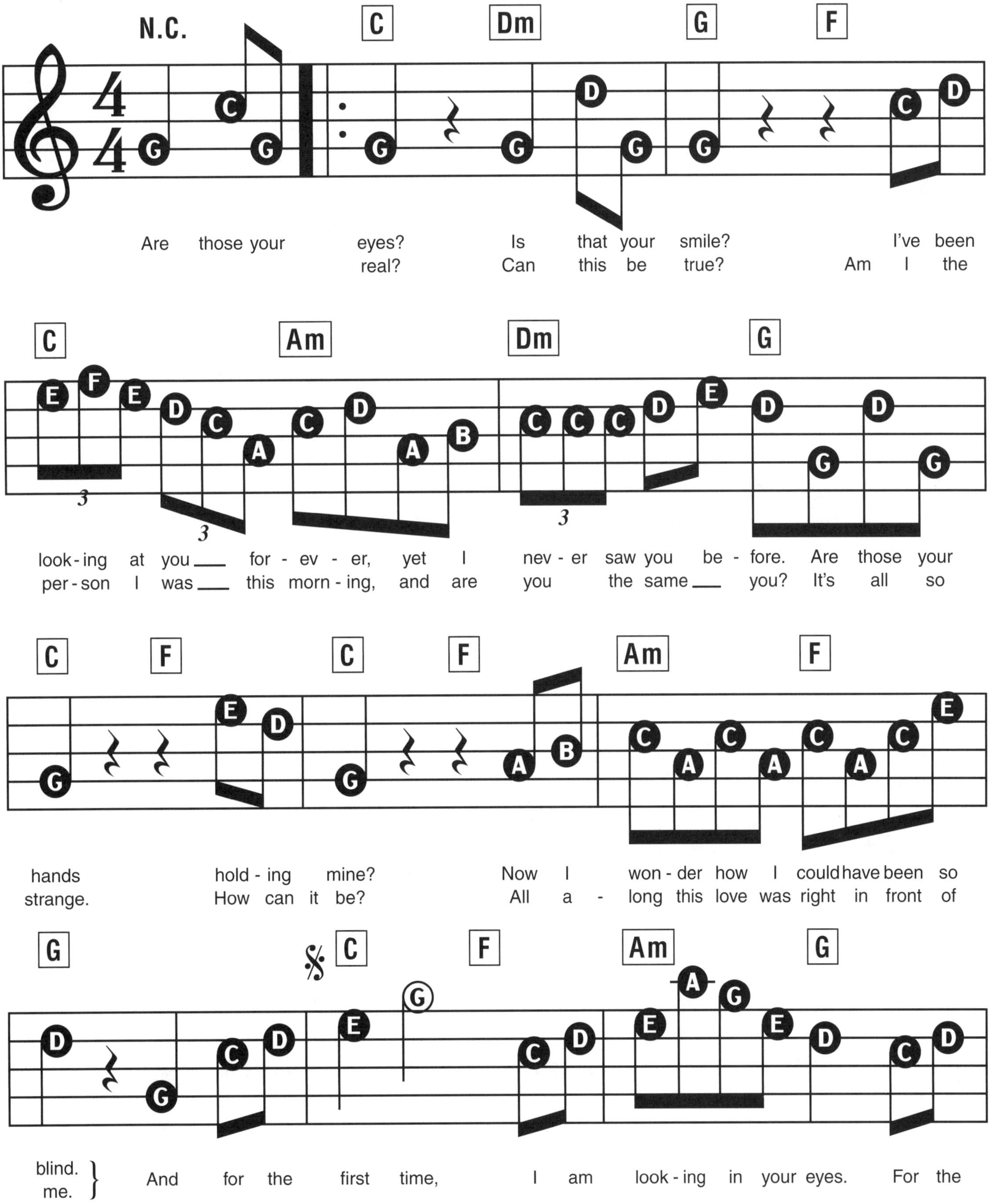
N.C.
C Dm G F
Are those your eyes? Is that your smile? I've been
real? Can this be true? Am I the
C Am Dm G
look - ing at you ___ for - ev - er, yet I nev - er saw you be - fore. Are those your
per - son I was ___ this morn - ing, and are you the same ___ you? It's all so
C F C F Am F
hands hold - ing mine? Now I won - der how I could have been so
strange. How can it be? All a - long this love was right in front of
G C F Am G
blind.
me.
And for the first time, I am look - ing in your eyes. For the

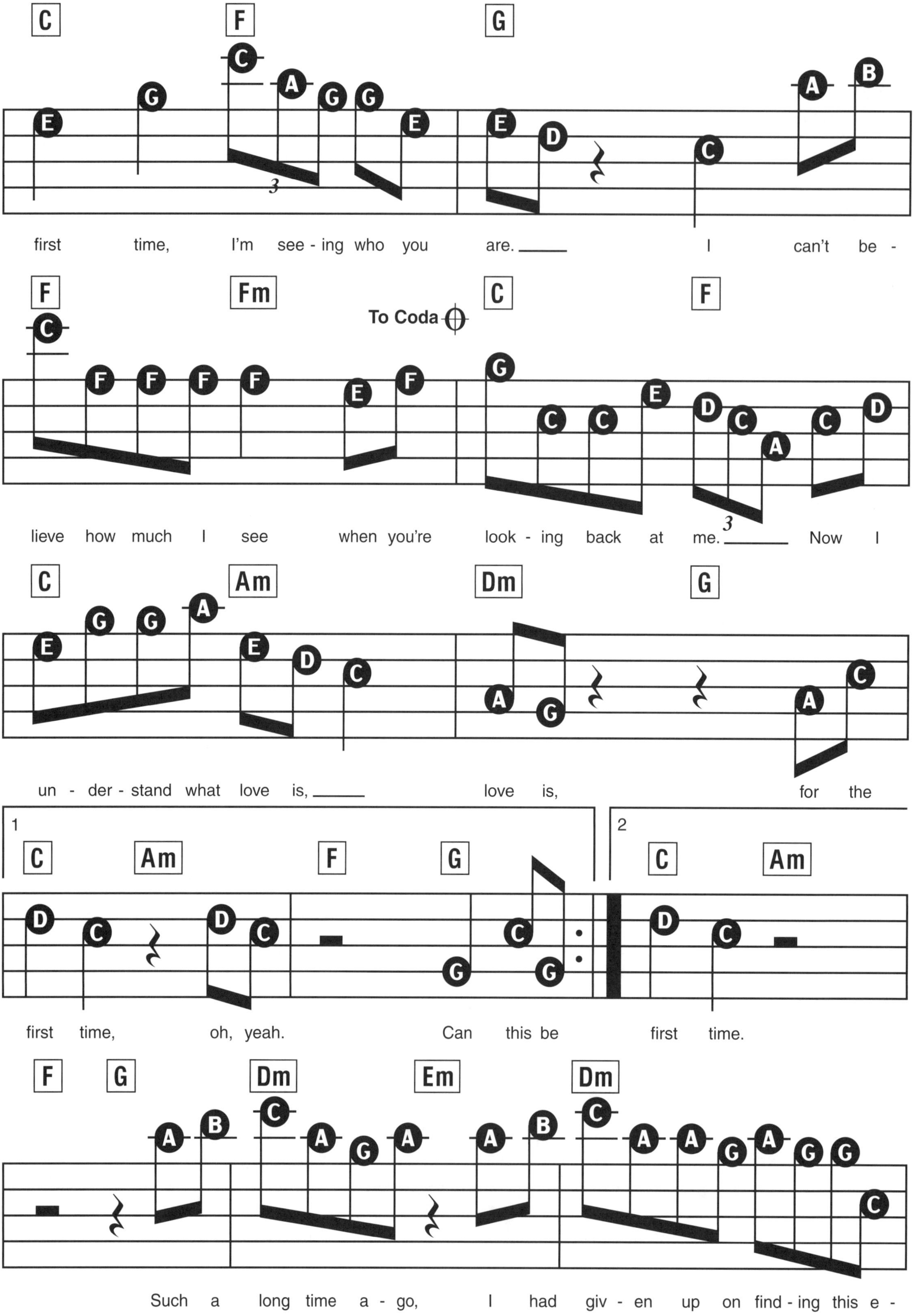
C F G
first time, I'm see - ing who you are. I can't be -
F Fm To Coda C F
lieve how much I see when you're look - ing back at me. Now I
C Am Dm G
un - der - stand what love is, love is, for the
1 C Am F G
first time, oh, yeah. Can this be
2 C Am
first time.
F G Dm Em Dm
Such a long time a - go, I had giv - en up on find - ing this e -

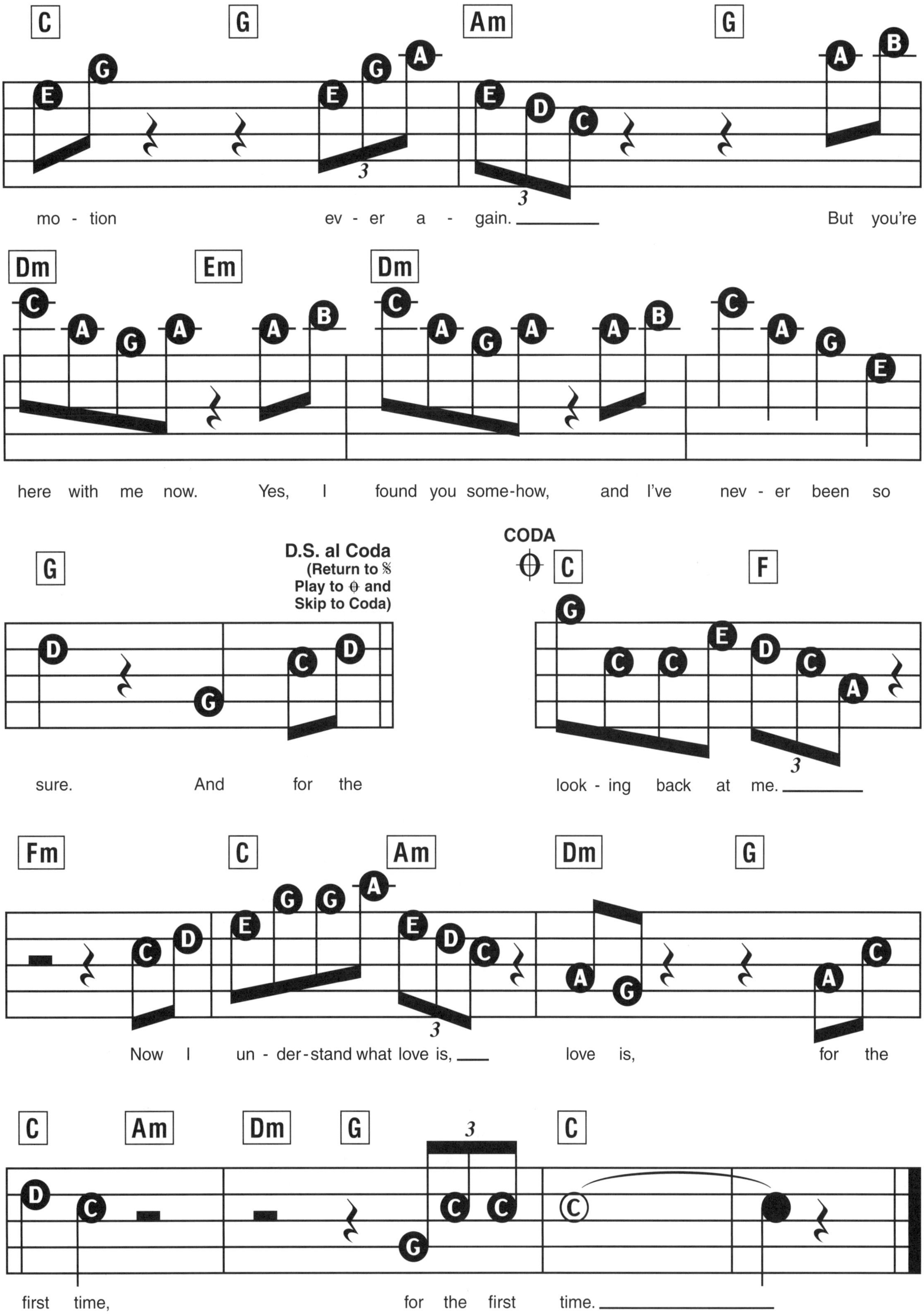
C G Am G
mo - tion ev - er a - gain. But you're
Dm Em Dm
here with me now. Yes, I found you some-how, and I've nev - er been so
G
sure. And for the
D.S. al Coda
(Return to 𝄋
Play to ⊕ and
Skip to Coda)
CODA
C F
look - ing back at me.
Fm C Am Dm G
Now I un - der-stand what love is, love is, for the
C Am Dm G C
first time, for the first time.

A Fine Romance
from SWING TIME

Registration 2
Rhythm: Ballad or Swing

Words by Dorothy Fields
Music by Jerome Kern

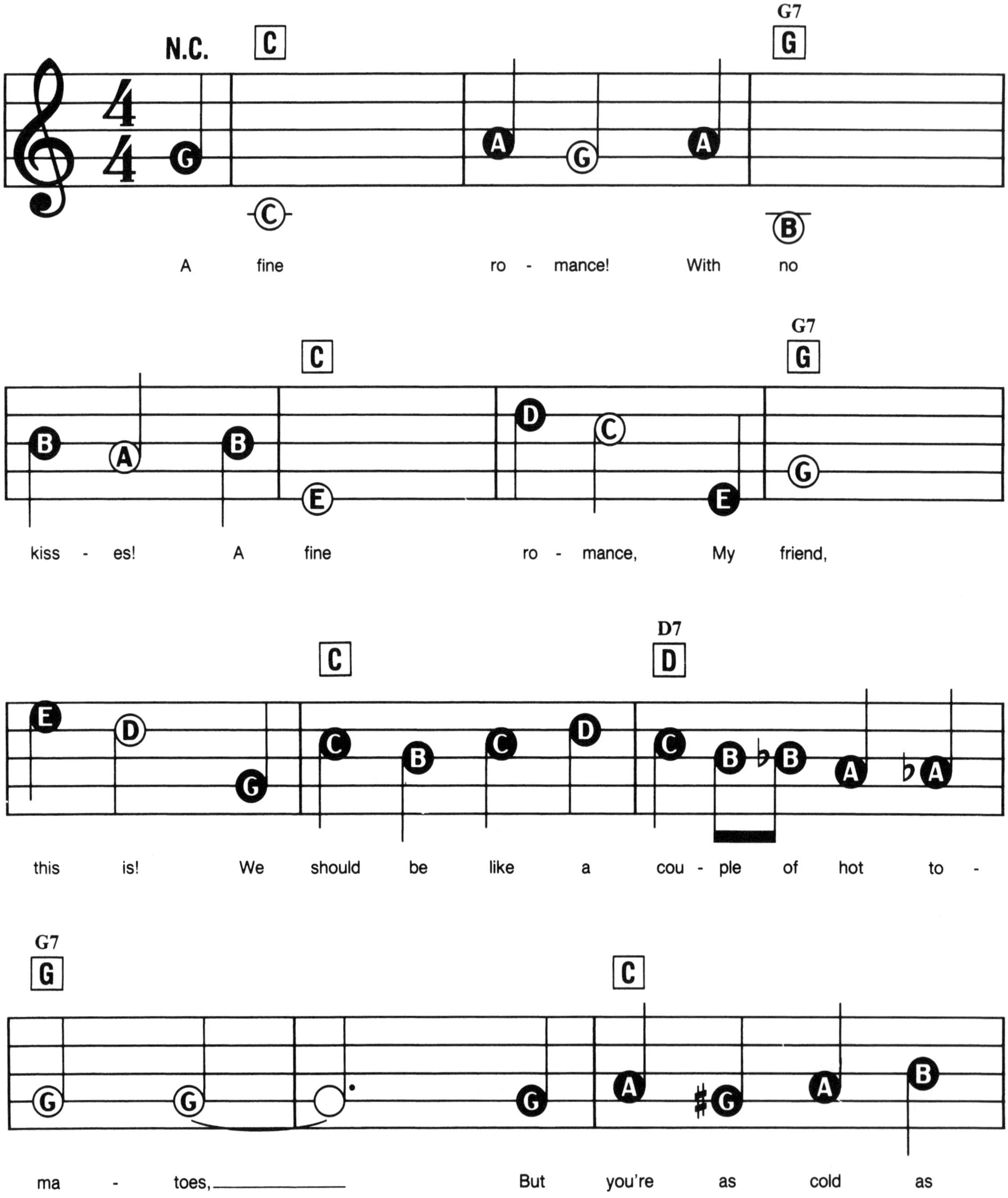
N.C.
C
G7
G
A fine romance! With no
kiss - es! A fine romance, My friend,
D7
D
this is! We should be like a cou - ple of hot to -
ma - toes,
But you're as cold as

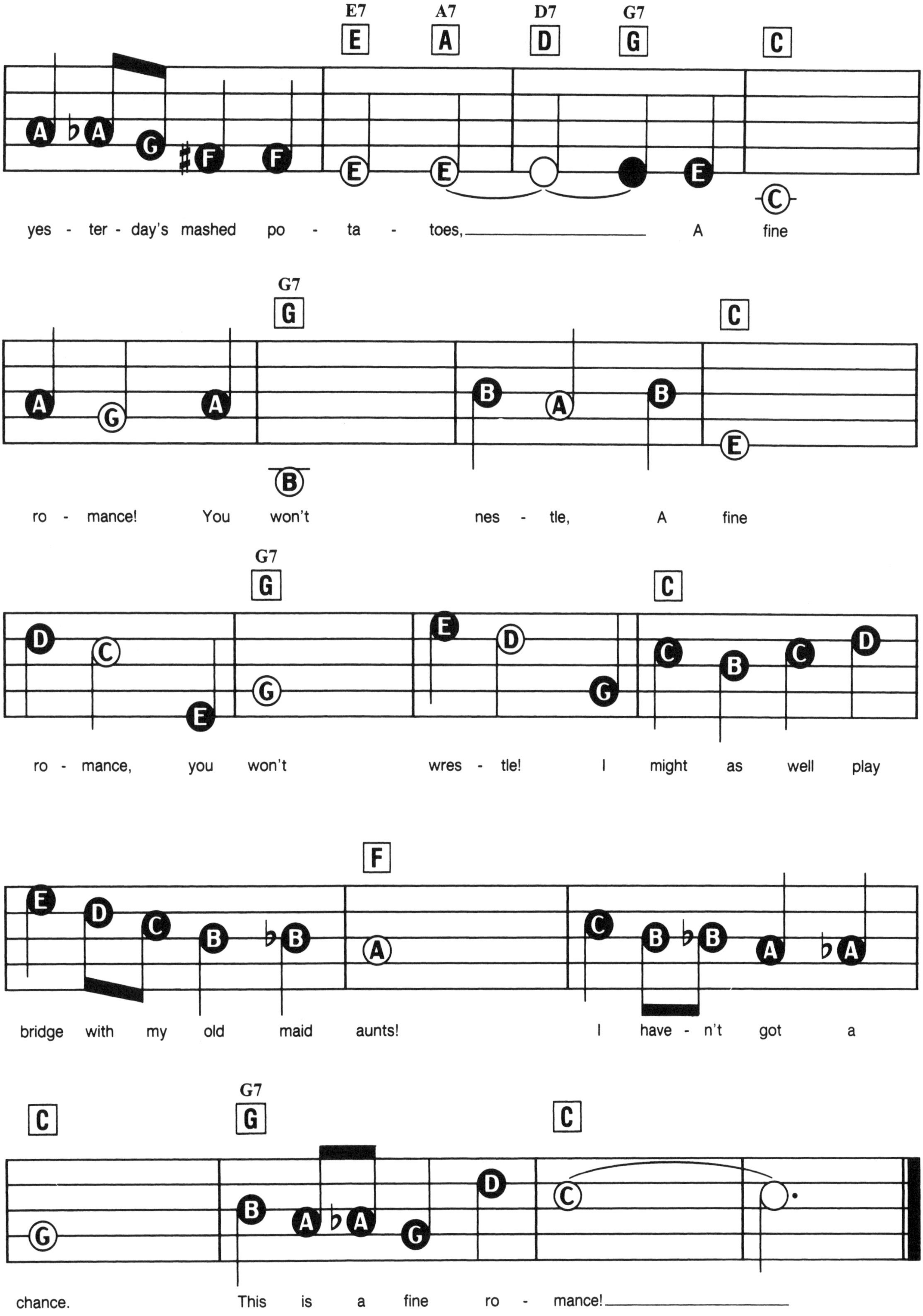
E7 A7 D7 G7
E A D G C
yes - ter - day's mashed po - ta - toes, A fine
G7
G C
ro - mance! You won't nes - tle, A fine
G7
G C
ro - mance, you won't wres - tle! I might as well play
F
bridge with my old maid aunts! I have - n't got a
G7
C G C
chance. This is a fine ro - mance!

I Will Wait for You

from THE UMBRELLAS OF CHERBOURG

Registration 9
Rhythm: Fox Trot or Swing

Music by Michel Legrand
Original French Text by Jacques Demy
English Words by Norman Gimbel

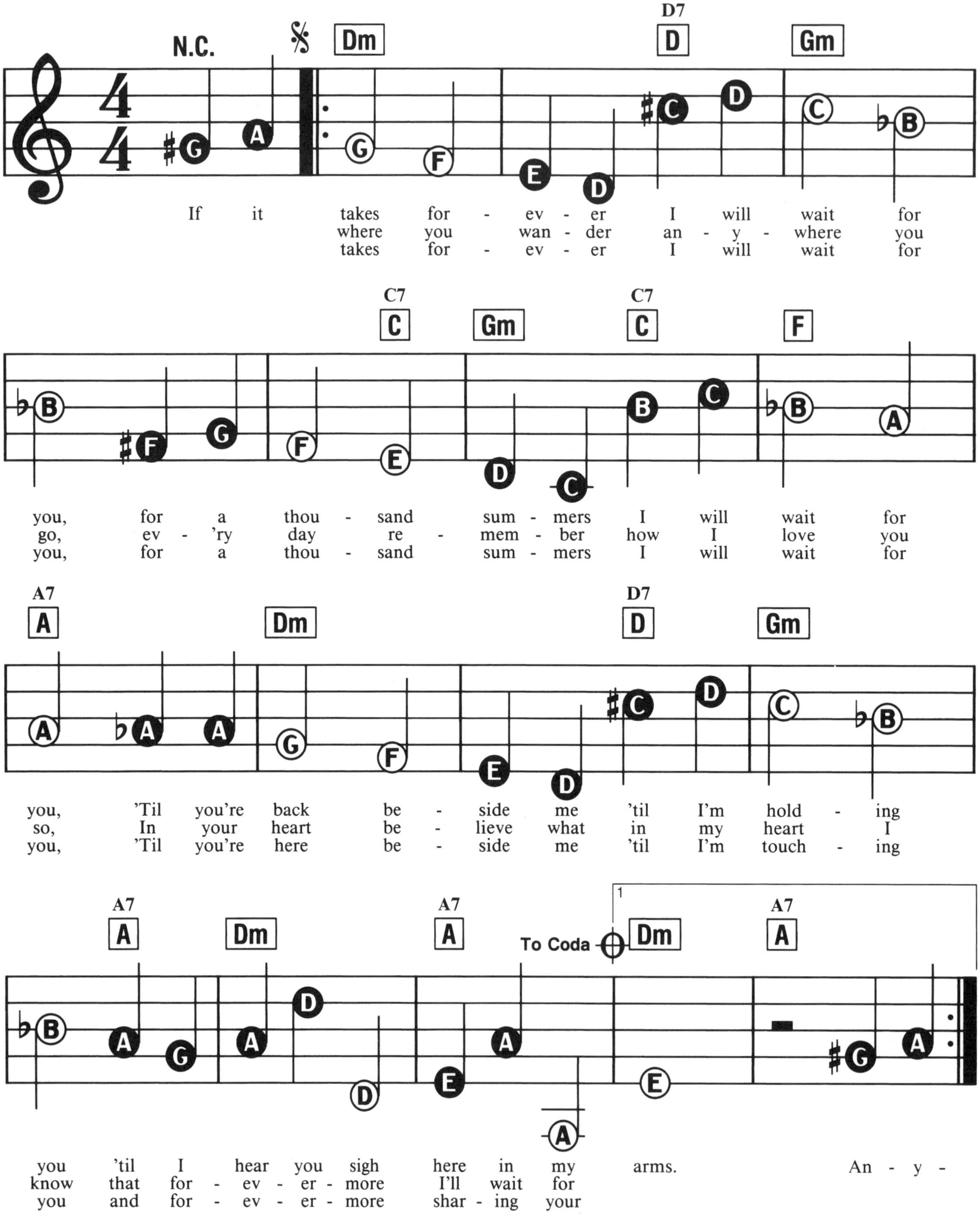
N.C.
Dm
D7
D
Gm
#G A G F E D #C D C bB
If it takes for - ev - er I will wait for
where you wan - der an - y - where you
takes for - ev - er I will wait for
C7
C
Gm
C7
C
F
bB #F G F E D C B C bB A
you, for a thou - sand sum - mers I will wait for
go, ev - 'ry day re - mem - ber how I love you
you, for a thou - sand sum - mers I will wait for
A7
A
Dm
D7
D
Gm
A bA A G F E D #C D C bB
you, 'Til you're back be - side me 'til I'm hold - ing
so, In your heart be - lieve what in my heart I
you, 'Til you're here be - side me 'til I'm touch - ing
A7
A
Dm
A7
A
To Coda
Dm
A7
A
1
bB A G A D D E A A E #G A
you 'til I hear you sigh here in my arms. An - y -
know that for - ev - er - more I'll wait for
you and for - ev - er - more shar - ing your

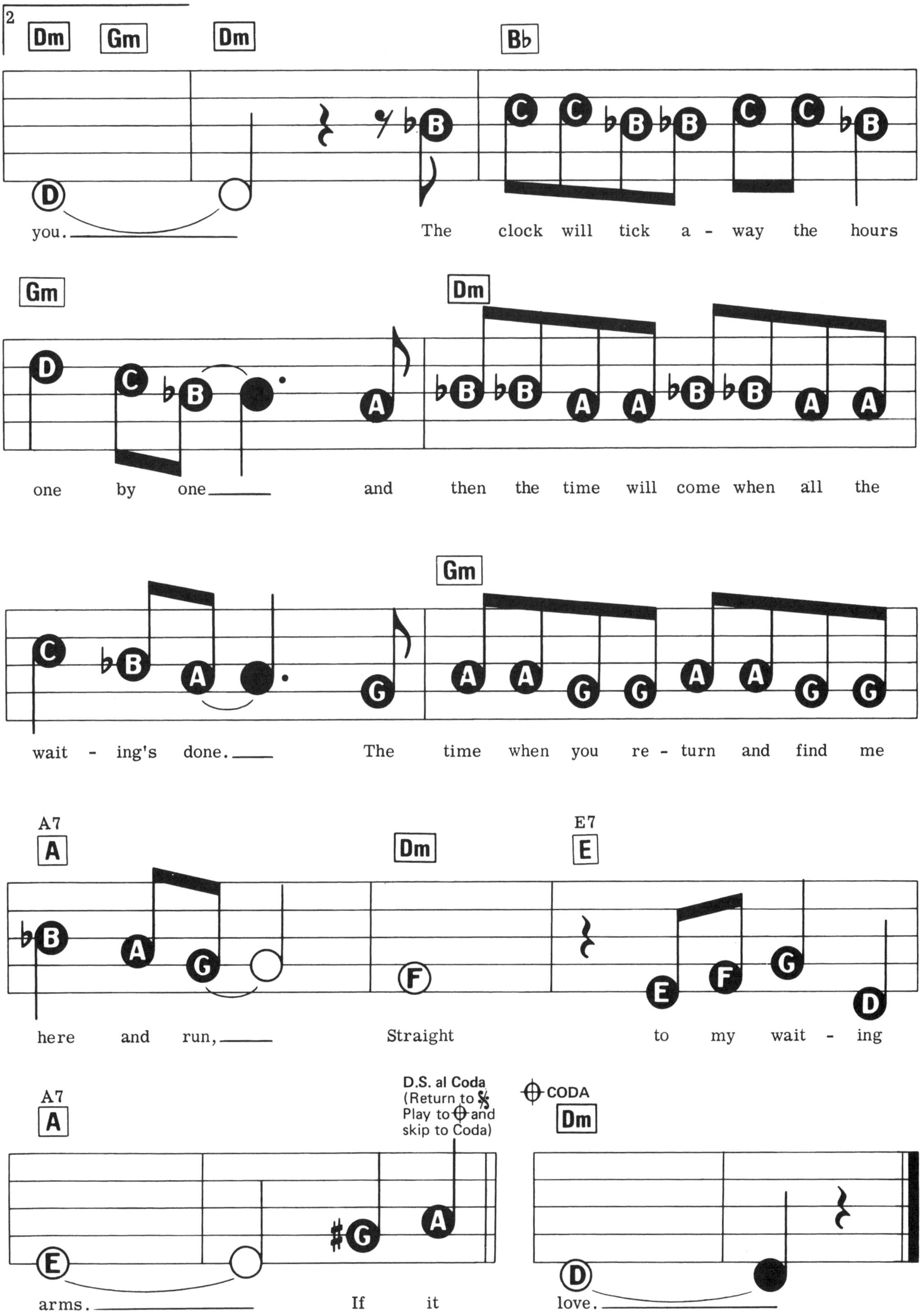
2
Dm Gm Dm Bb
you. The clock will tick a - way the hours
Gm Dm
one by one and then the time will come when all the
Gm
wait - ing's done. The time when you re - turn and find me
A7 A Dm E7 E
here and run, Straight to my wait - ing
A7 A
arms. If it
D.S. al Coda (Return to 𝄋 Play to ⊕ and skip to Coda)
⊕ CODA
Dm
love.

I'll Be There For You

Registration 9
Rhythm: Rock or 8-Beat

Words and Music by Jon Bon Jovi
and Richie Sambora

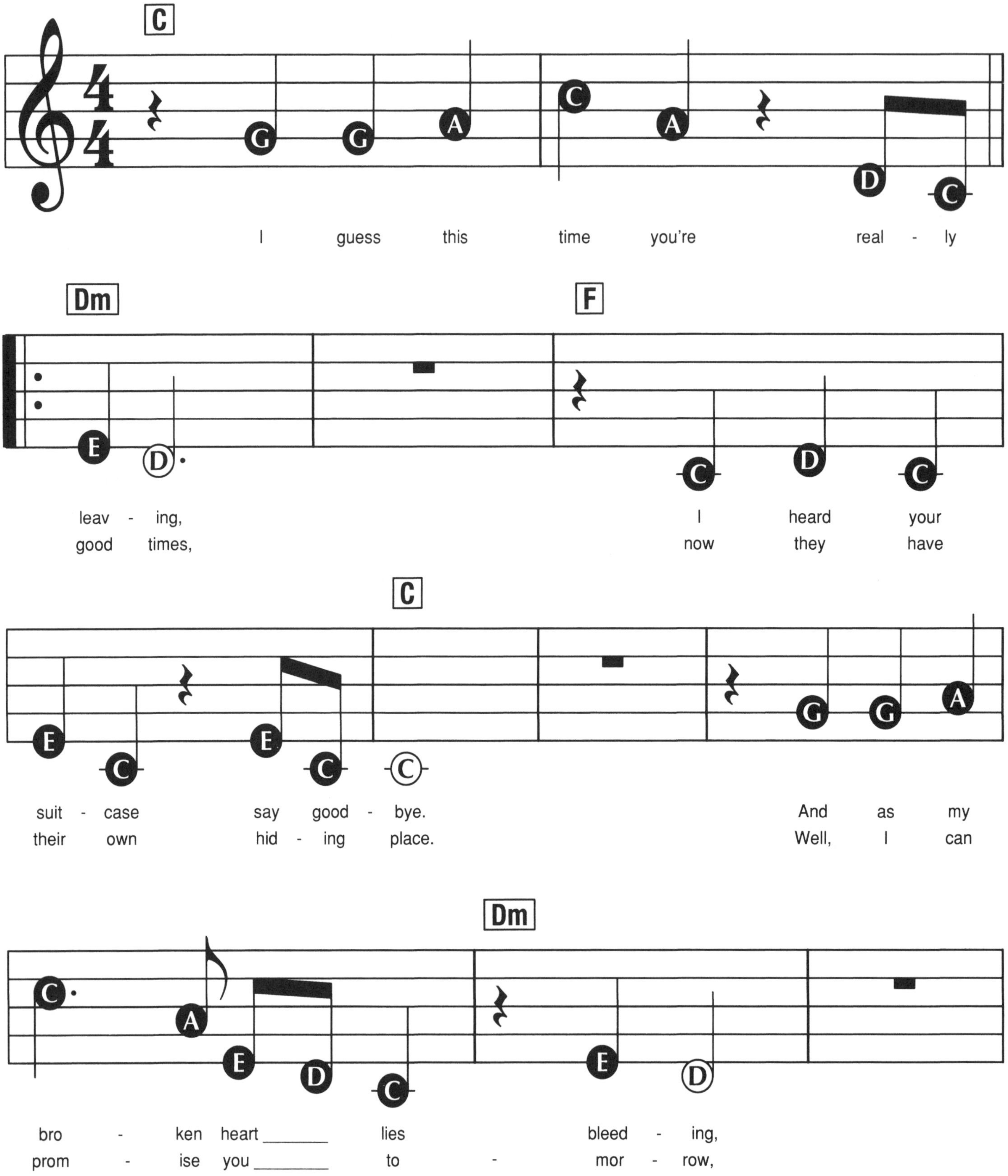
C
I guess this time you're real - ly
Dm
F
leav - ing, I heard your
good times, now they have
C
suit - case say good - bye. And as my
their own hid - ing place. Well, I can
Dm
bro - ken heart ______ lies bleed - ing,
prom - ise you ______ to - mor - row,

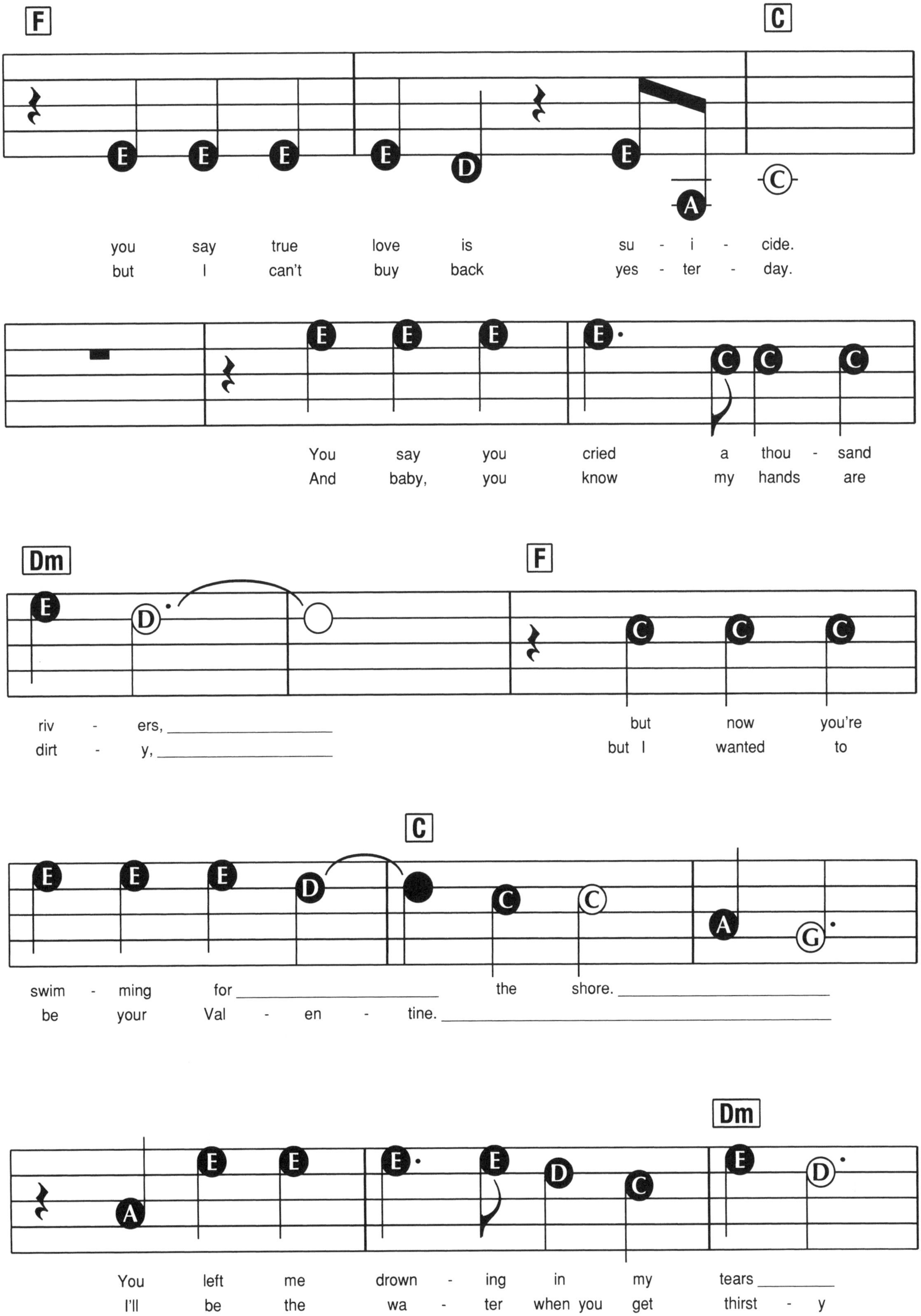
F
C
you say true love is su - i - cide.
but I can't buy back yes - ter - day.
You say you cried a thou - sand
And baby, you know my hands are
Dm
F
riv - ers,
dirt - y,
but now you're
but I wanted to
C
swim - ming for the shore.
be your Val - en - tine.
Dm
You left me drown - ing in my tears
I'll be the wa - ter when you get thirst - y

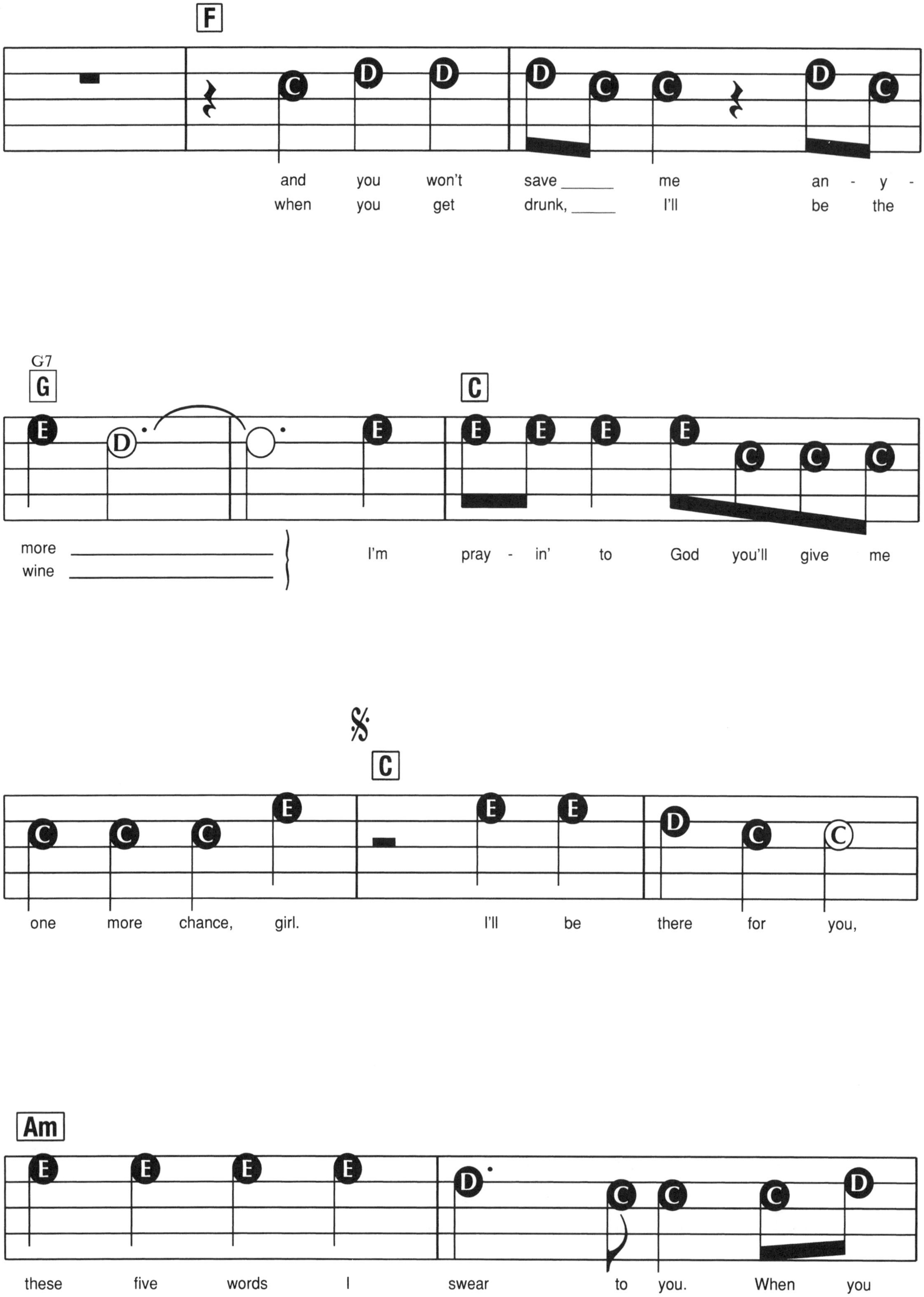
F
and you won't save ______ me an - y -
when you get drunk, ______ I'll be the
G7
G
C
more
wine
I'm pray - in' to God you'll give me
C
one more chance, girl. I'll be there for you,
Am
these five words I swear to you. When you

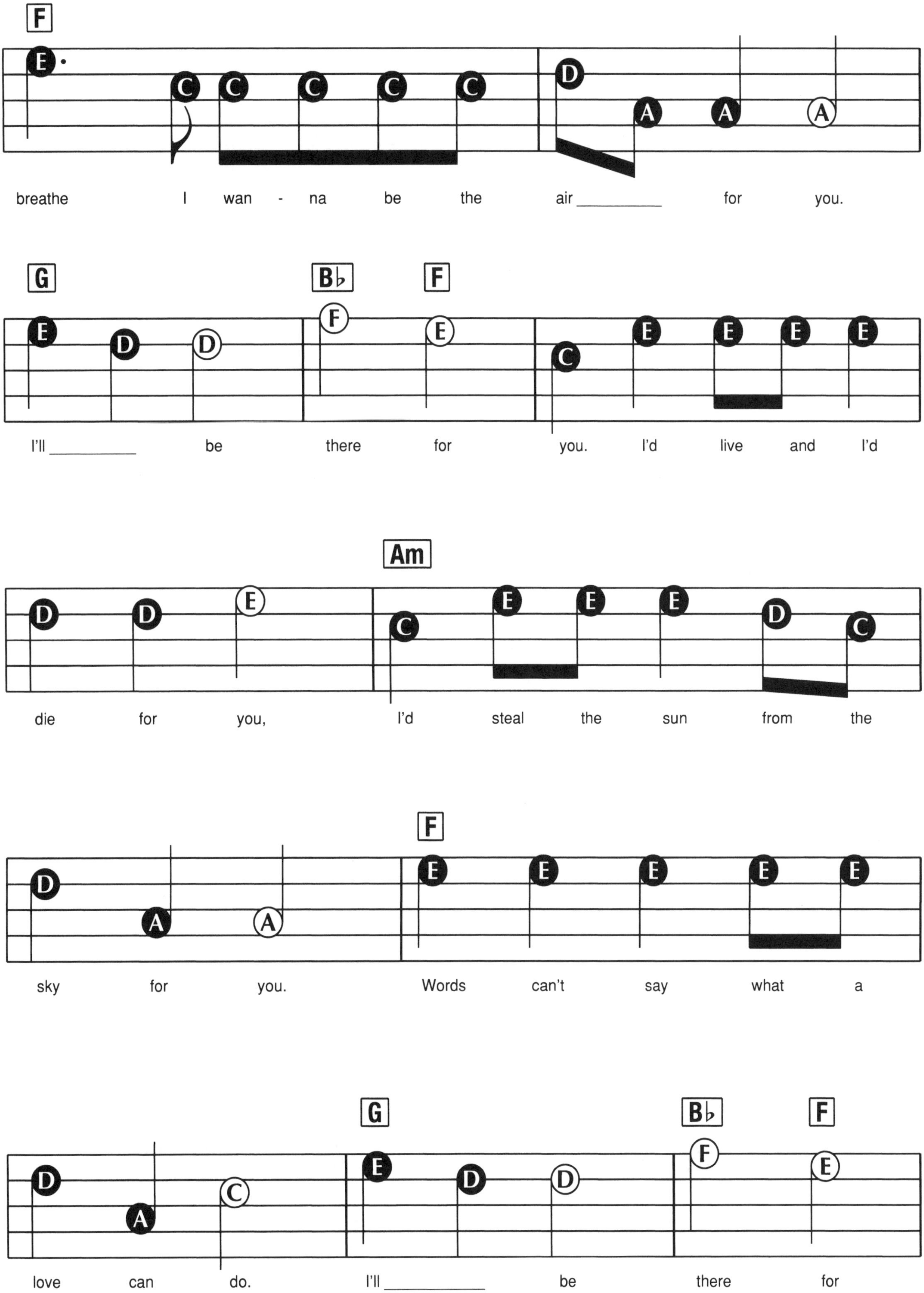
F
breathe I wan - na be the air for you.
G Bb F
I'll be there for you. I'd live and I'd
Am
die for you, I'd steal the sun from the
F
sky for you. Words can't say what a
G Bb F
love can do. I'll be there for

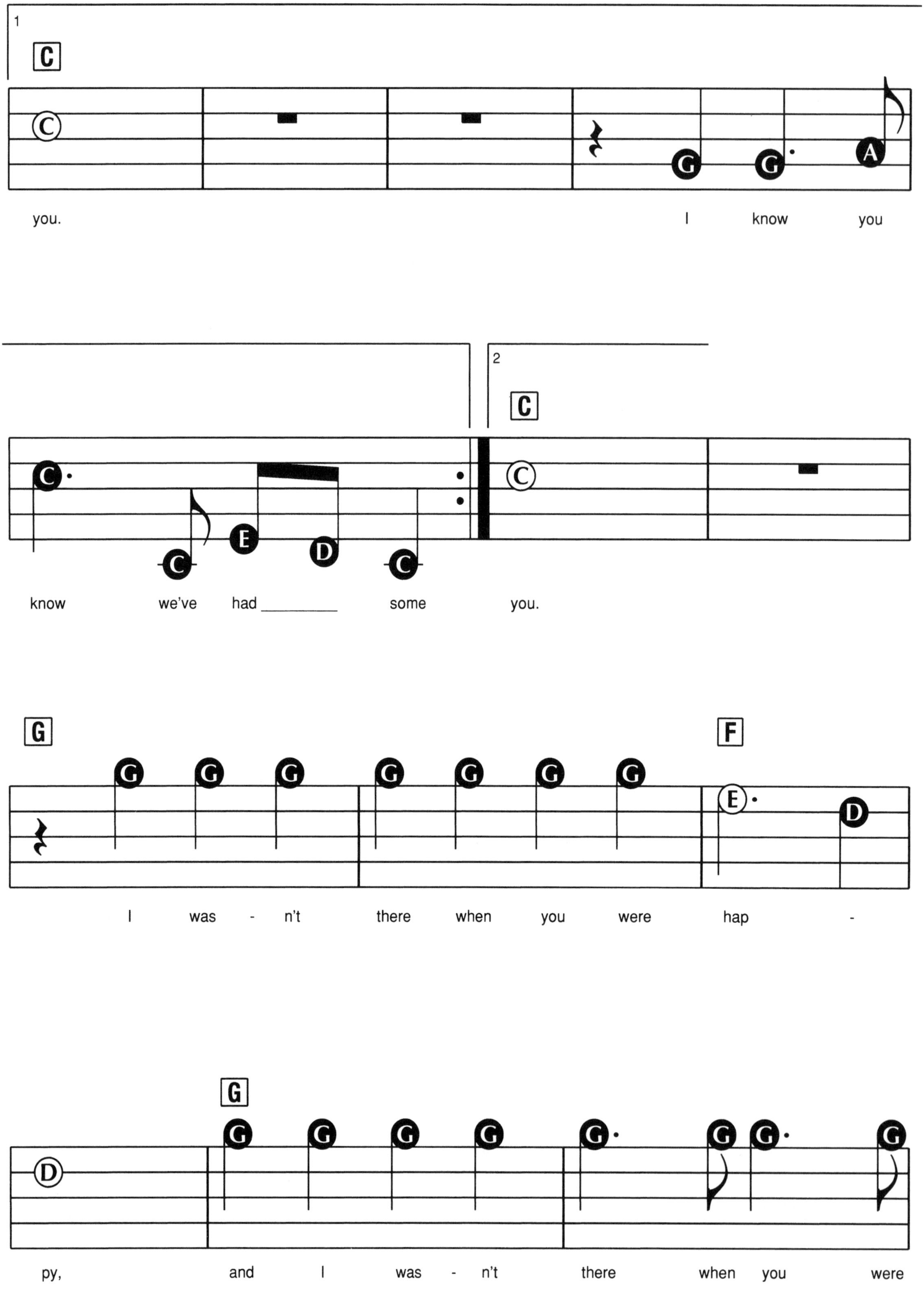
1
C
you.
I know you
know we've had ________ some
2
C
you.
G
I was - n't there when you were
F
hap - py,
G
and I was - n't there when you were

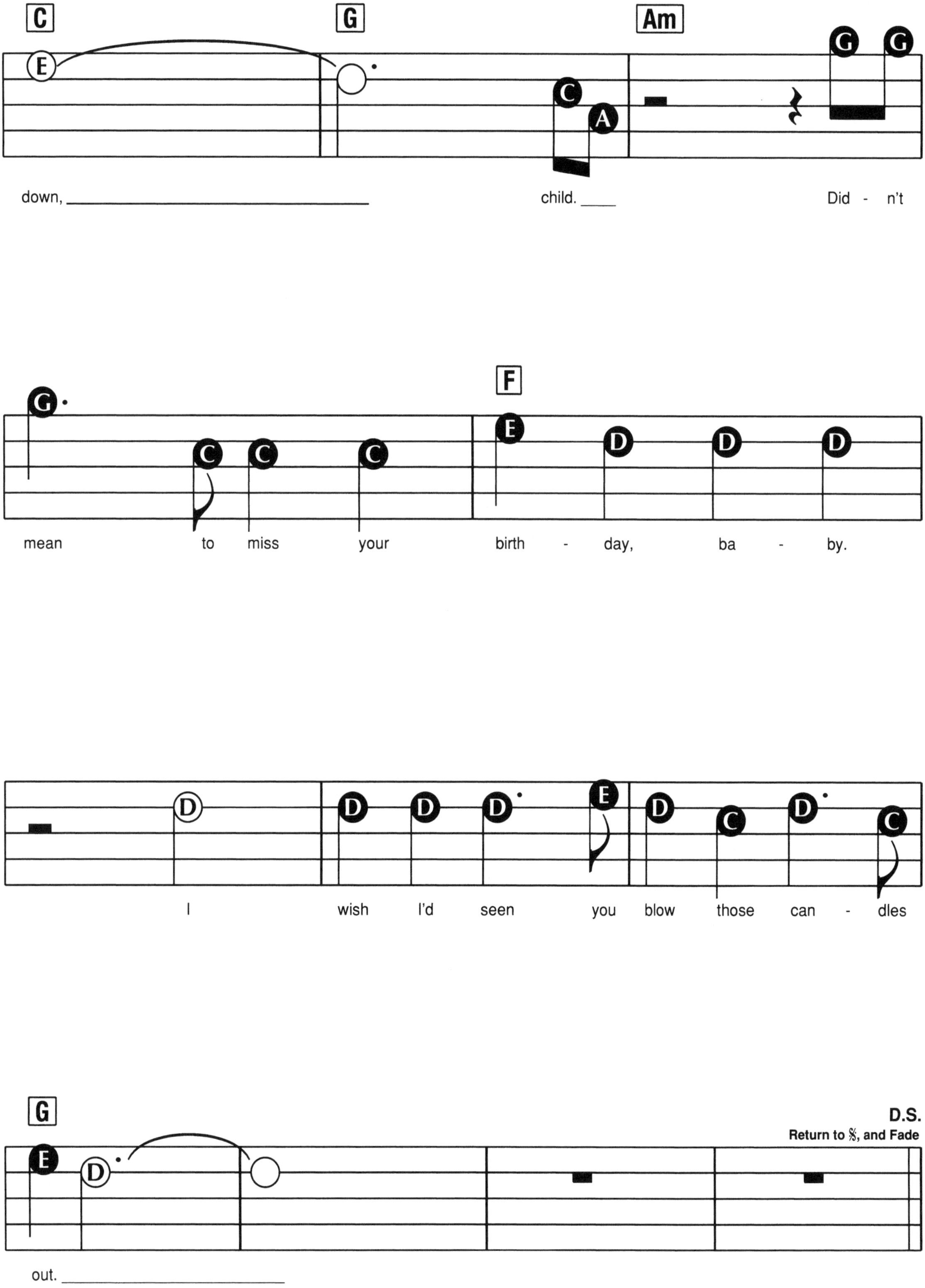
C G Am
down, child. Did - n't
mean to miss your birth - day, ba - by.
F
I wish I'd seen you blow those can - dles
G
out.
D.S.
Return to 𝄋, and Fade

I've Told Ev'ry Little Star

from MUSIC IN THE AIR

Registration 8
Rhythm: Ballad or Swing

Lyrics by Oscar Hammerstein II
Music by Jerome Kern

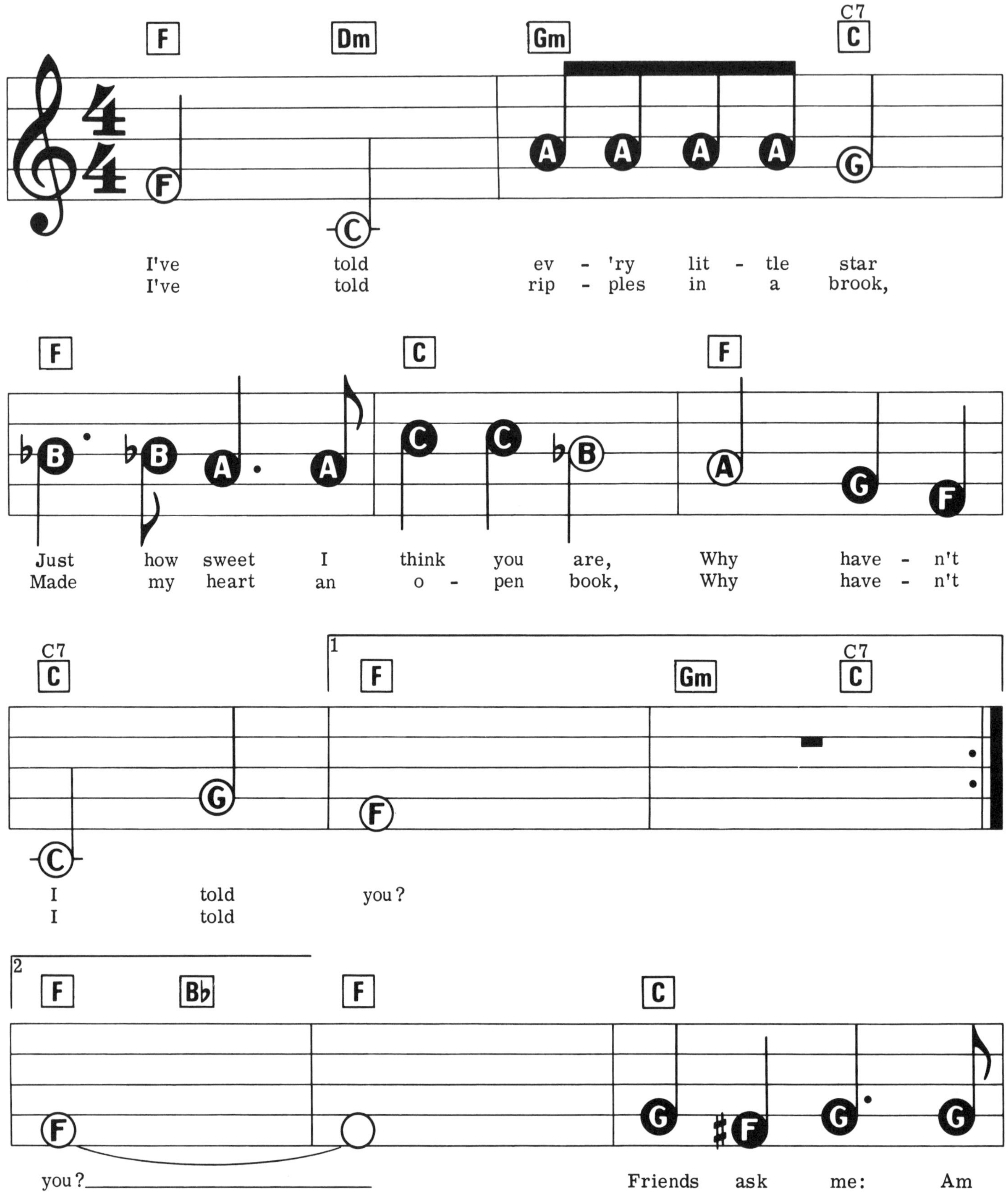
F Dm Gm C7 C
I've told ev - 'ry lit - tle star
I've told rip - ples in a brook,
F C F
Just how sweet I think you are, Why have - n't
Made my heart an o - pen book, Why have - n't
C7 C
I told you?
I told
1 F Gm C7 C
2 F Bb F C
you?
Friends ask me: Am

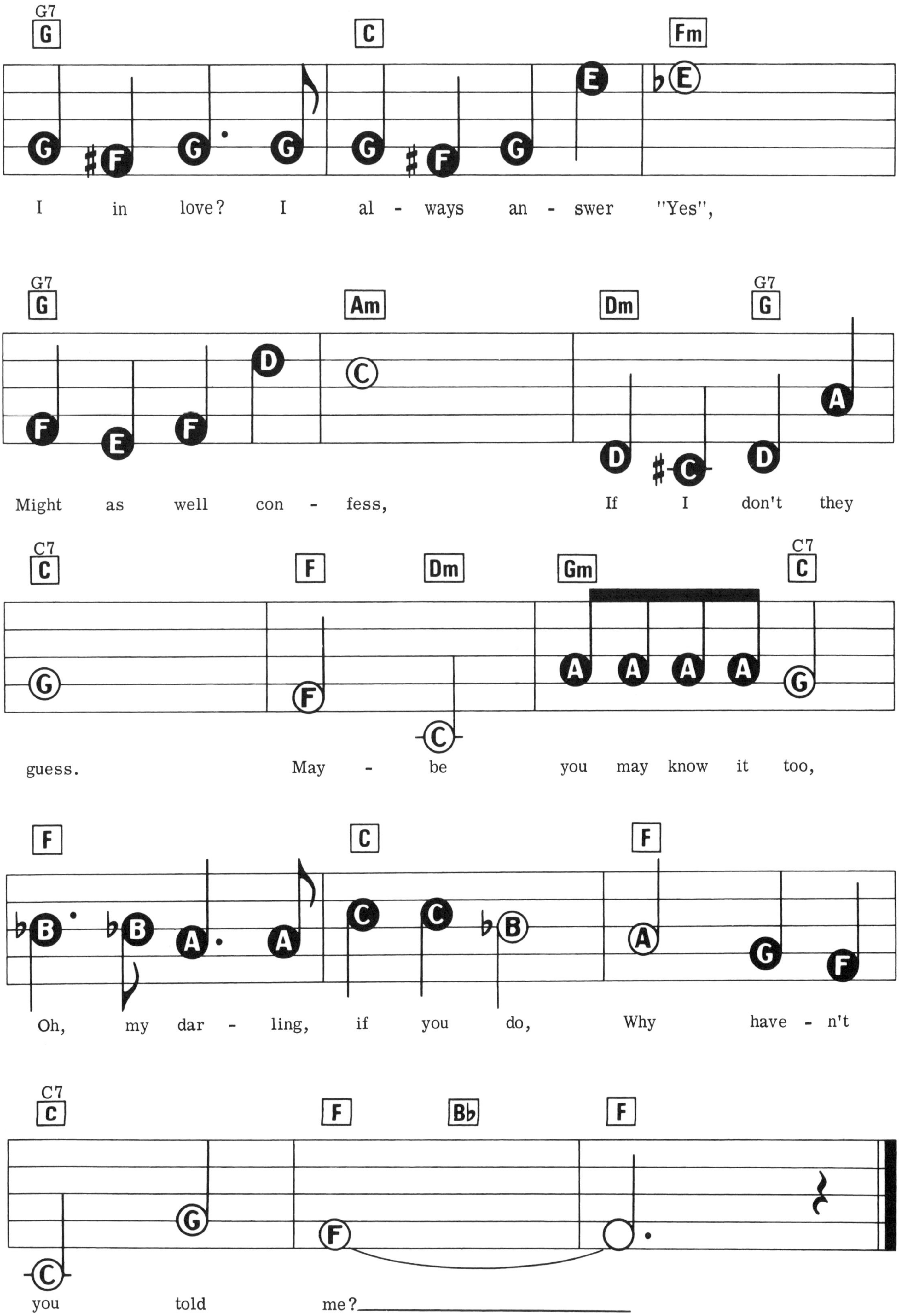
G7 G C Fm
I in love? I al - ways an - swer "Yes",
G7 G Am Dm G7 G
Might as well con - fess, If I don't they
C7 C F Dm Gm C7 C
guess. May - be you may know it too,
F C F
Oh, my dar - ling, if you do, Why have - n't
C7 C F B♭ F
you told me?

If I Loved You

from CAROUSEL

Registration 2
Rhythm: Ballad

Lyrics by Oscar Hammerstein II
Music by Richard Rodgers

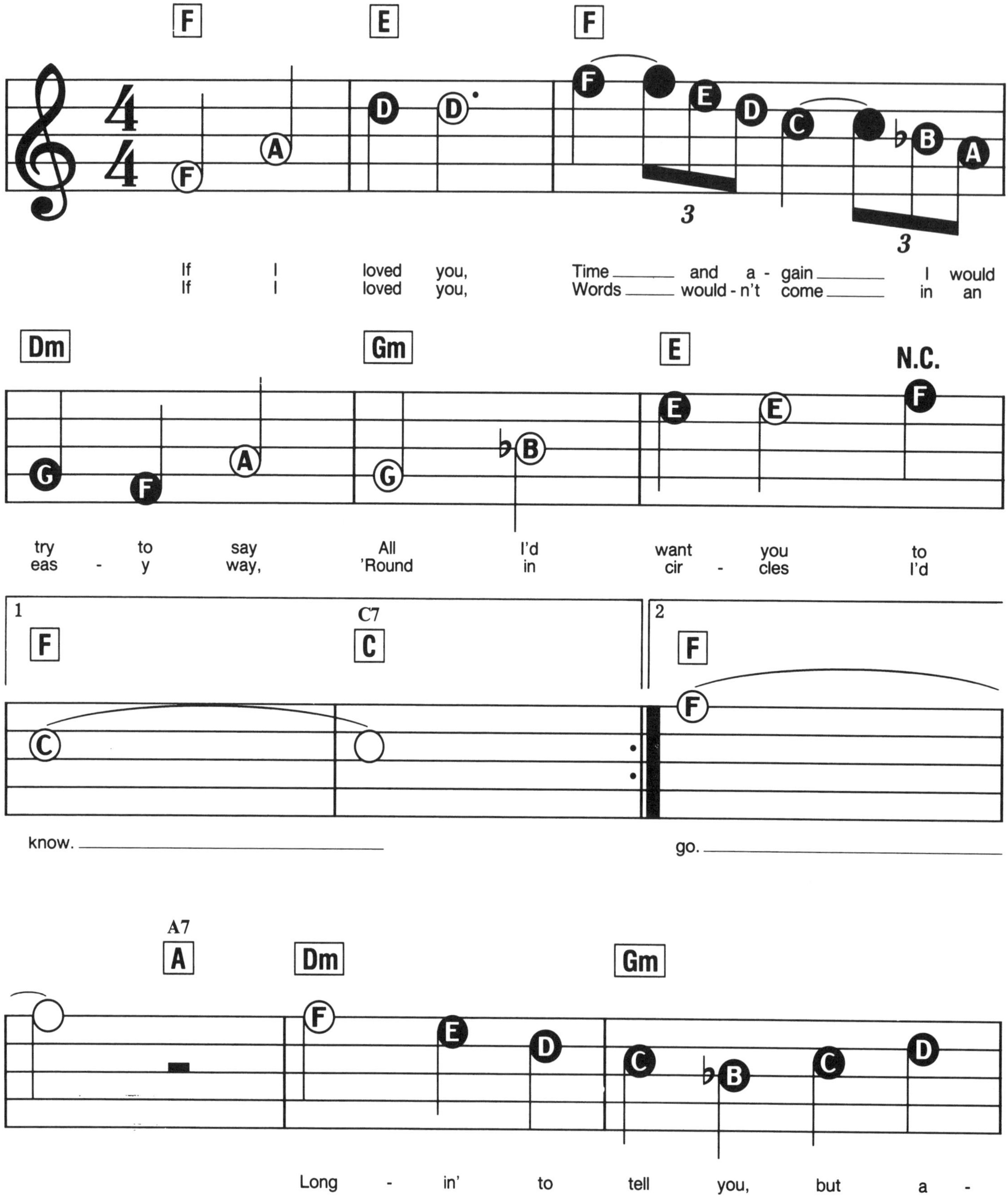
F
E
F
If I loved you, Time and a - gain I would
If I loved you, Words would - n't come in an
Dm
Gm
E
N.C.
try to say All I'd want you to
eas - y way, 'Round in cir - cles I'd
1
F
C7
C
know.
2
F
go.
A7
A
Dm
Gm
Long - in' to tell you, but a -

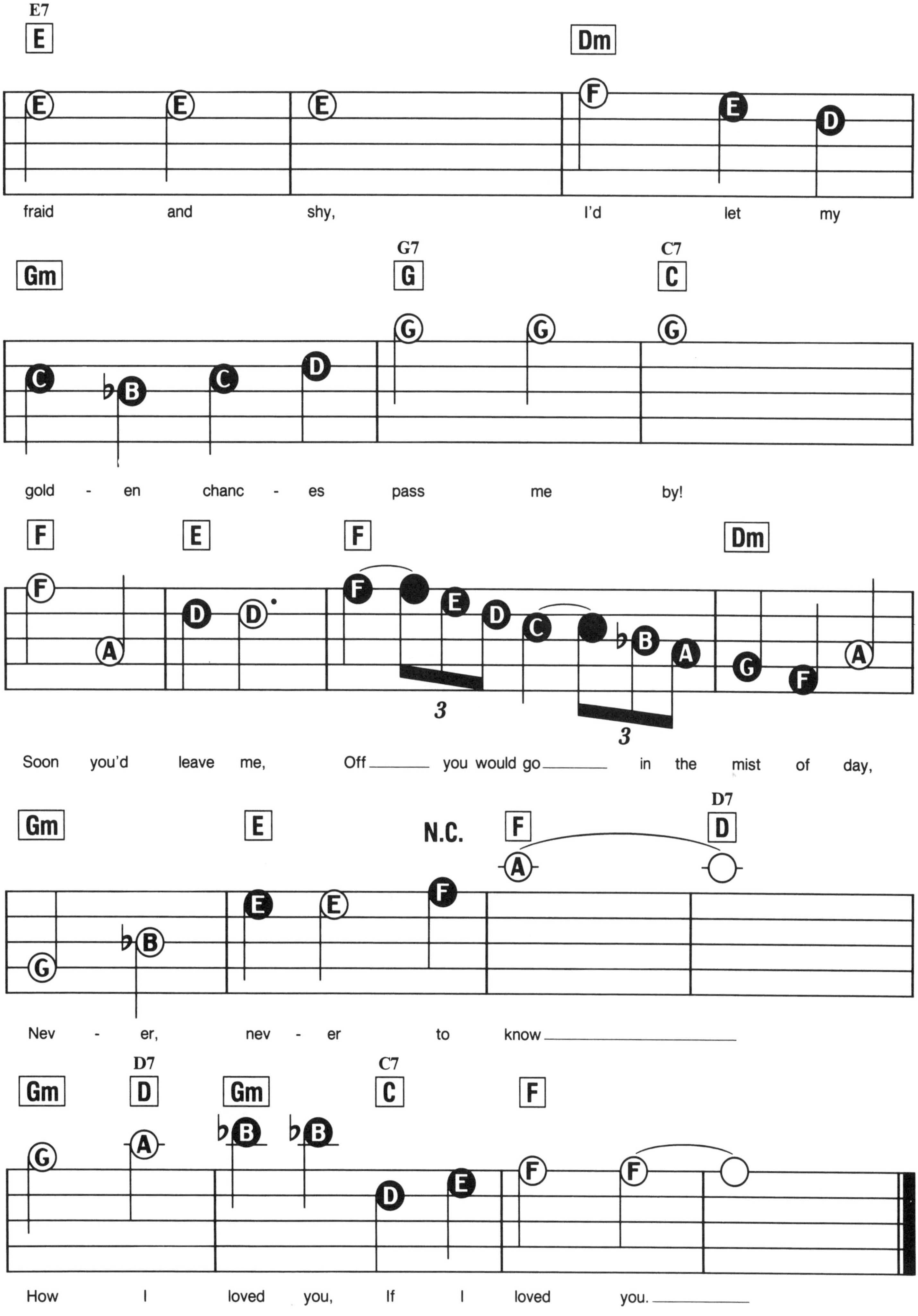
E7 E Dm
fraid and shy, I'd let my
Gm G7 G C7 C
gold - en chanc - es pass me by!
F E F Dm
Soon you'd leave me, Off you would go in the mist of day,
Gm E N.C. F D7 D
Nev - er, nev - er to know
Gm D7 D Gm C7 C F
How I loved you, If I loved you.

Isle of Capri

Registration 8
Rhythm: Bossa Nova or Latin

Words and Music by James Kennedy
and Wilhelm Grosz

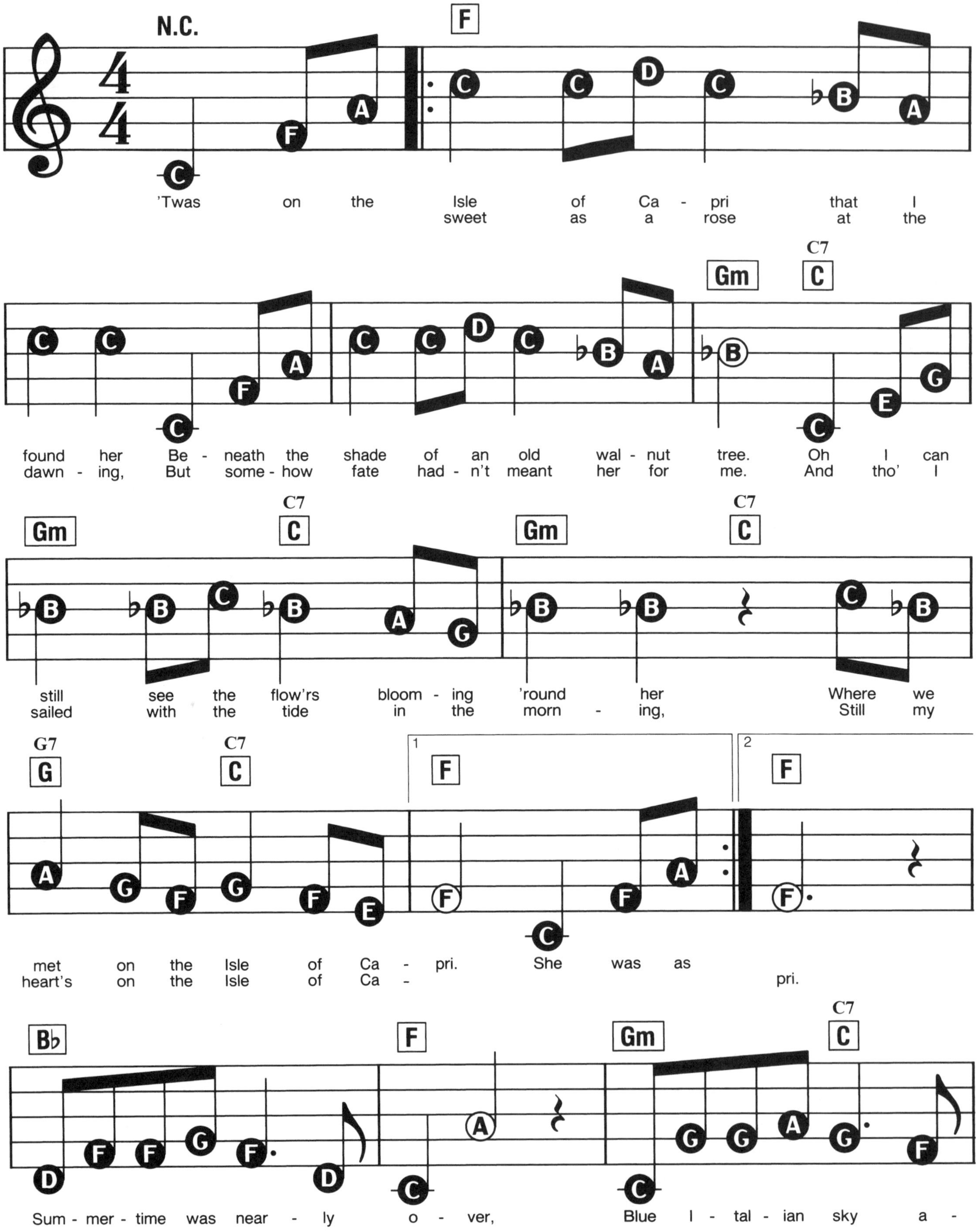
N.C.
F
'Twas on the Isle of Ca - pri that I
sweet as a rose at the
Gm C7 C
found her Be - neath the shade of an old wal - nut tree. Oh I can
dawn - ing, But some - how fate had - n't meant her for me. And tho' I
Gm C7 C Gm C7 C
still see the flow'rs bloom - ing 'round her Where we
sailed with the tide in the morn - ing, Still my
G7 G C7 C 1 F 2 F
met on the Isle of Ca - pri. She was as
heart's on the Isle of Ca - pri.
B♭ F Gm C7 C
Sum - mer - time was near - ly o - ver, Blue I - tal - ian sky a -

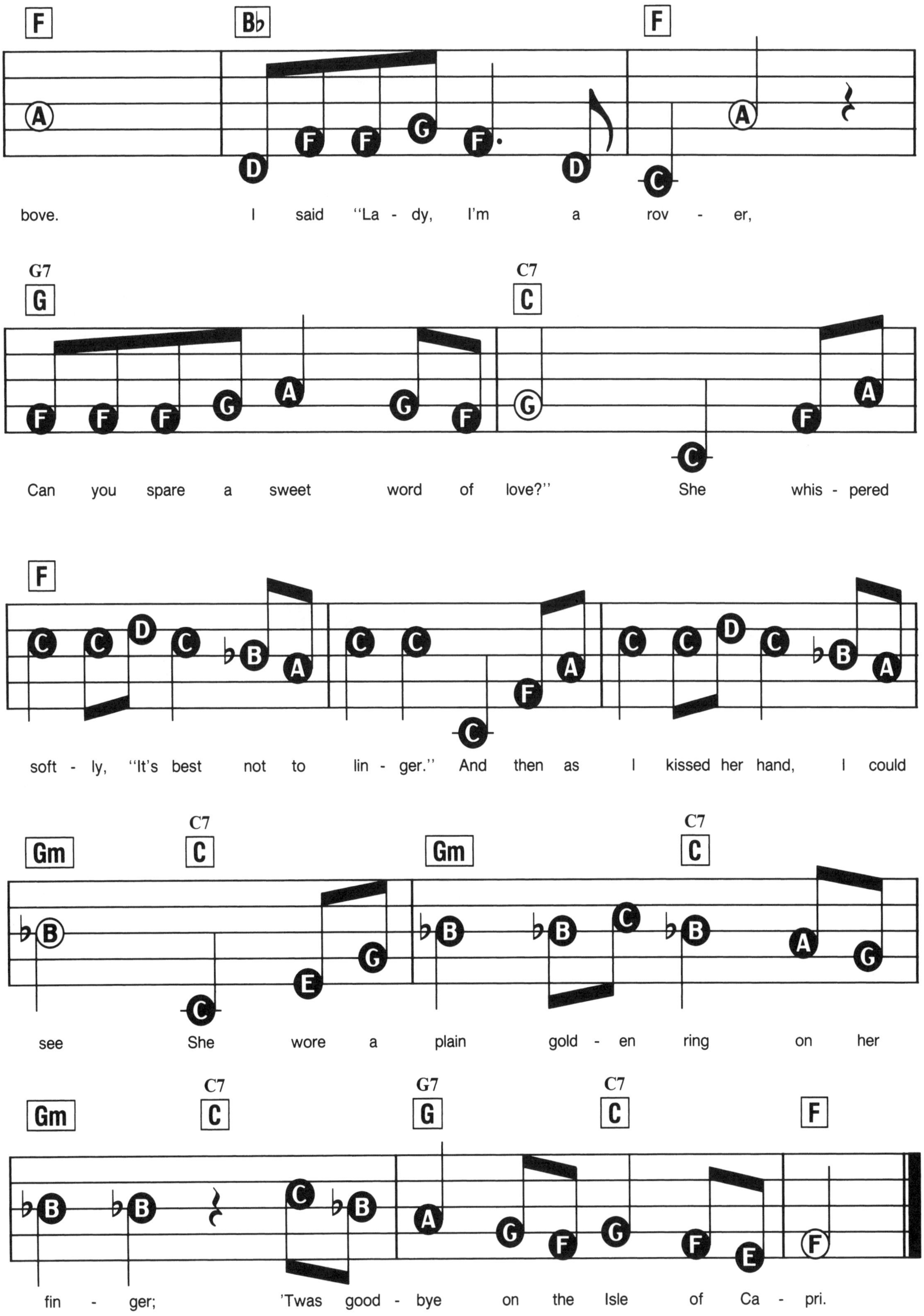
F Bb F
bove. I said "La - dy, I'm a rov - er,
G7 G C7 C
Can you spare a sweet word of love?" She whis - pered
F
soft - ly, "It's best not to lin - ger." And then as I kissed her hand, I could
Gm C7 C Gm C7 C
see She wore a plain gold - en ring on her
Gm C7 C G7 G C7 C F
fin - ger; 'Twas good - bye on the Isle of Ca - pri.

The Last Time I Saw Paris

from LADY, BE GOOD
from TILL THE CLOUDS ROLL BY

Registration 10
Rhythm: Ballad or Swing

Lyrics by Oscar Hammerstein II
Music by Jerome Kern

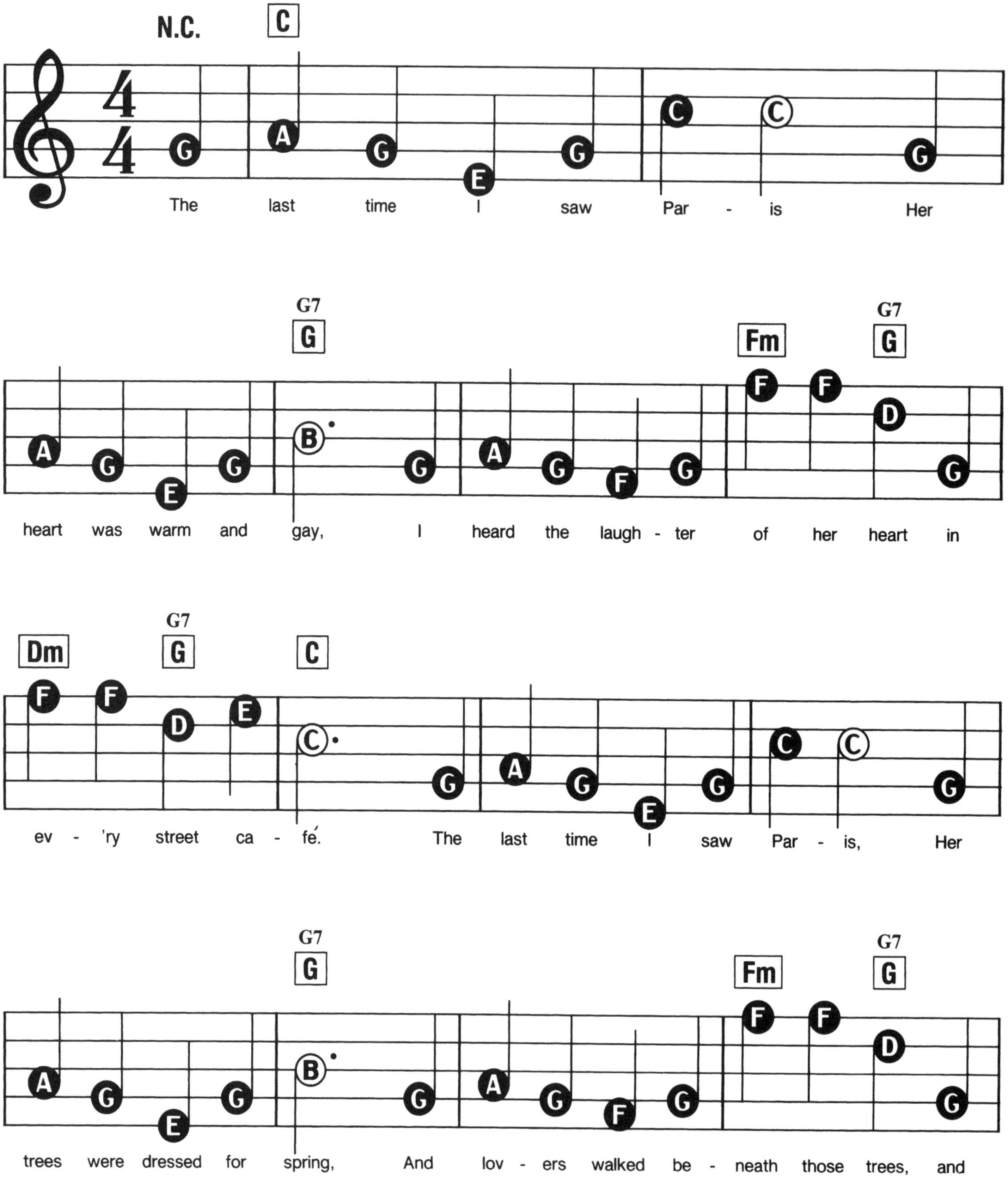
N.C.
C
The last time I saw Par - is Her
G7 G Fm G7 G
heart was warm and gay, I heard the laugh - ter of her heart in
Dm G7 G C
ev - 'ry street ca - fé. The last time I saw Par - is, Her
G7 G Fm G7 G
trees were dressed for spring, And lov - ers walked be - neath those trees, and

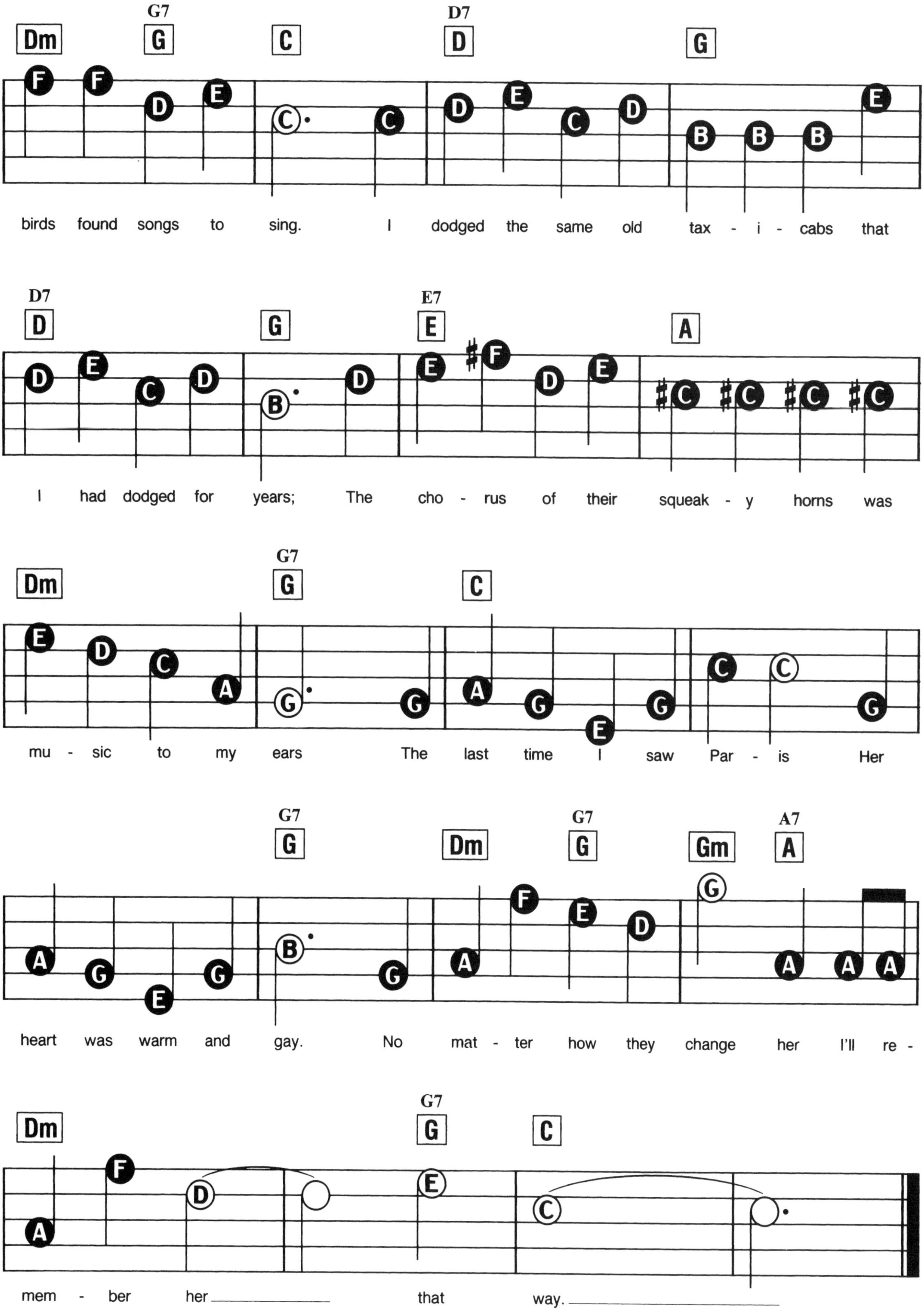
Dm G7 G C D7 D G
birds found songs to sing. I dodged the same old tax - i - cabs that
D7 D G E7 E A
I had dodged for years; The cho - rus of their squeak - y horns was
Dm G7 G C
mu - sic to my ears The last time I saw Par - is Her
G7 G Dm G7 G Gm A7 A
heart was warm and gay. No mat - ter how they change her I'll re -
Dm G7 G C
mem - ber her that way.

Let's Stay Together

Registration 7
Rhythm: 4/4 Ballad or R&B

Words and Music by Al Green,
Willie Mitchell and Al Jackson, Jr.

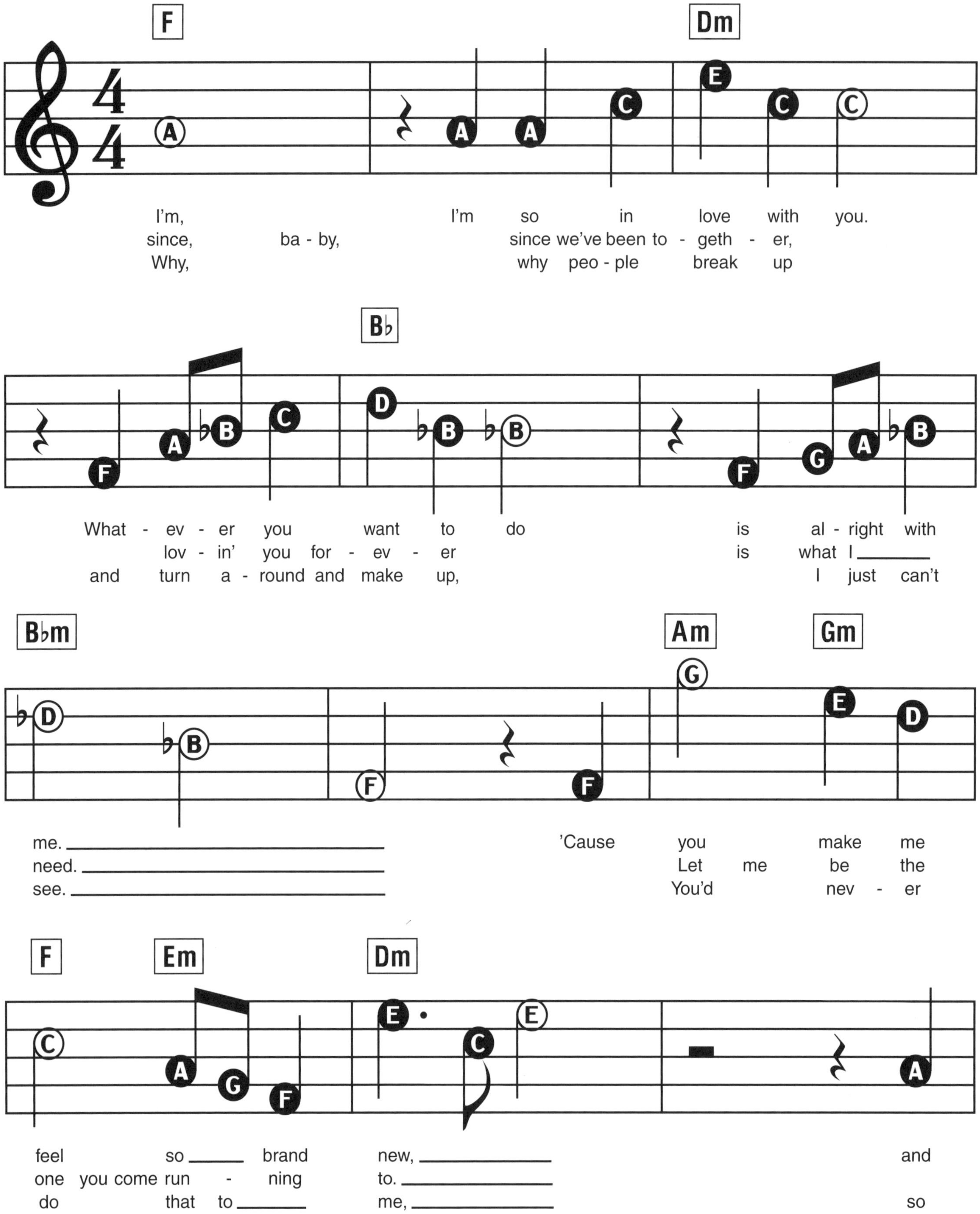
F
Dm
I'm, I'm so in love with you.
since, ba - by, since we've been to - geth - er,
Why, why peo - ple break up
B♭
What - ev - er you want to do is al - right with
lov - in' you for - ev - er is what I
and turn a - round and make up, I just can't
B♭m
Am
Gm
me. 'Cause you make me
need. Let me be the
see. You'd nev - er
F
Em
Dm
feel so brand new, and
one you come run - ning to.
do that to me, so

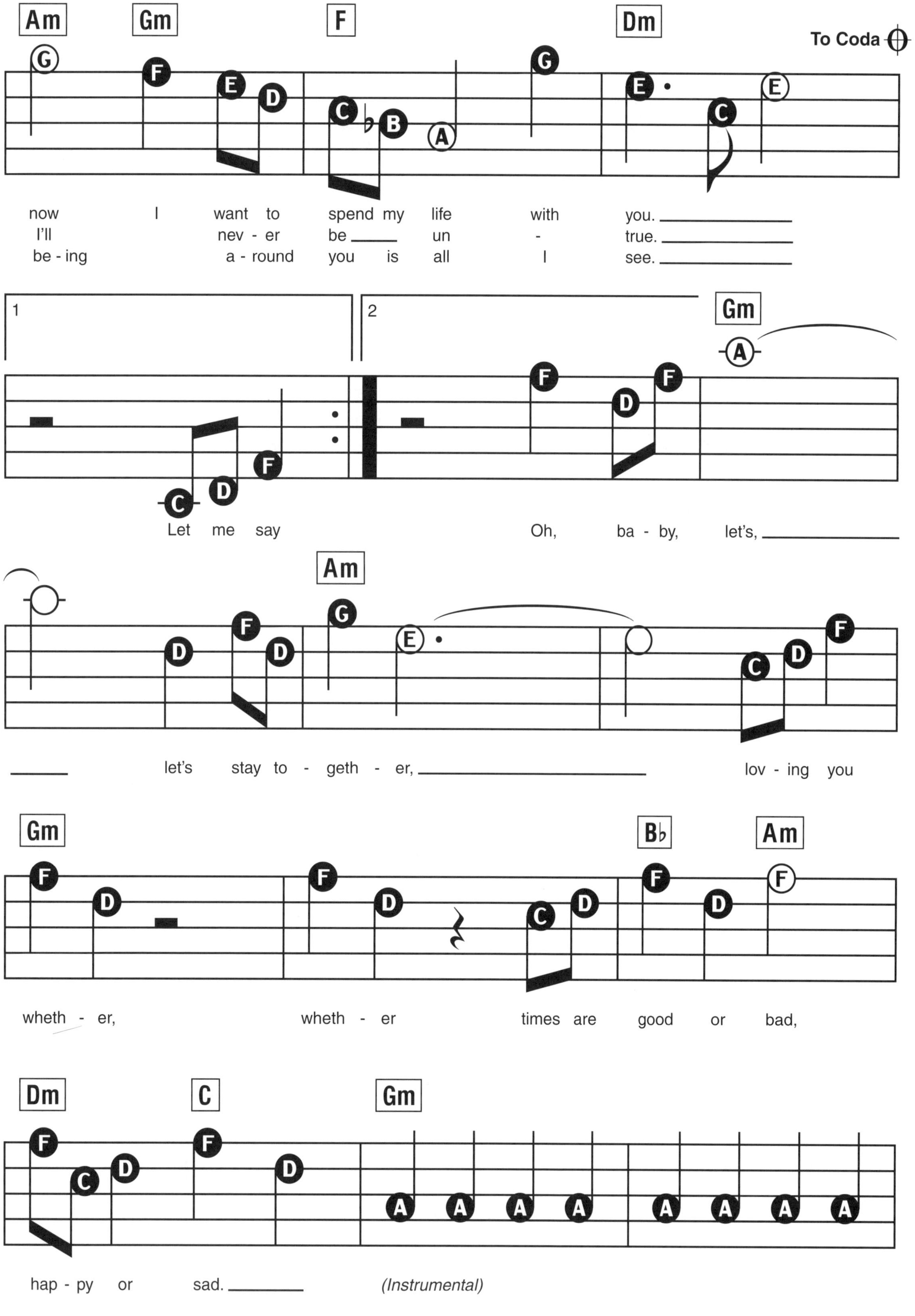
Am Gm F Dm
To Coda
now I want to spend my life with you.
I'll never - er be un - true.
be - ing a - round you is all I see.
1
2
Gm
Let me say
Oh, ba - by, let's,
Am
let's stay to - geth - er,
lov - ing you
Gm Bb Am
wheth - er, wheth - er times are good or bad,
Dm C Gm
hap - py or sad.
(Instrumental)

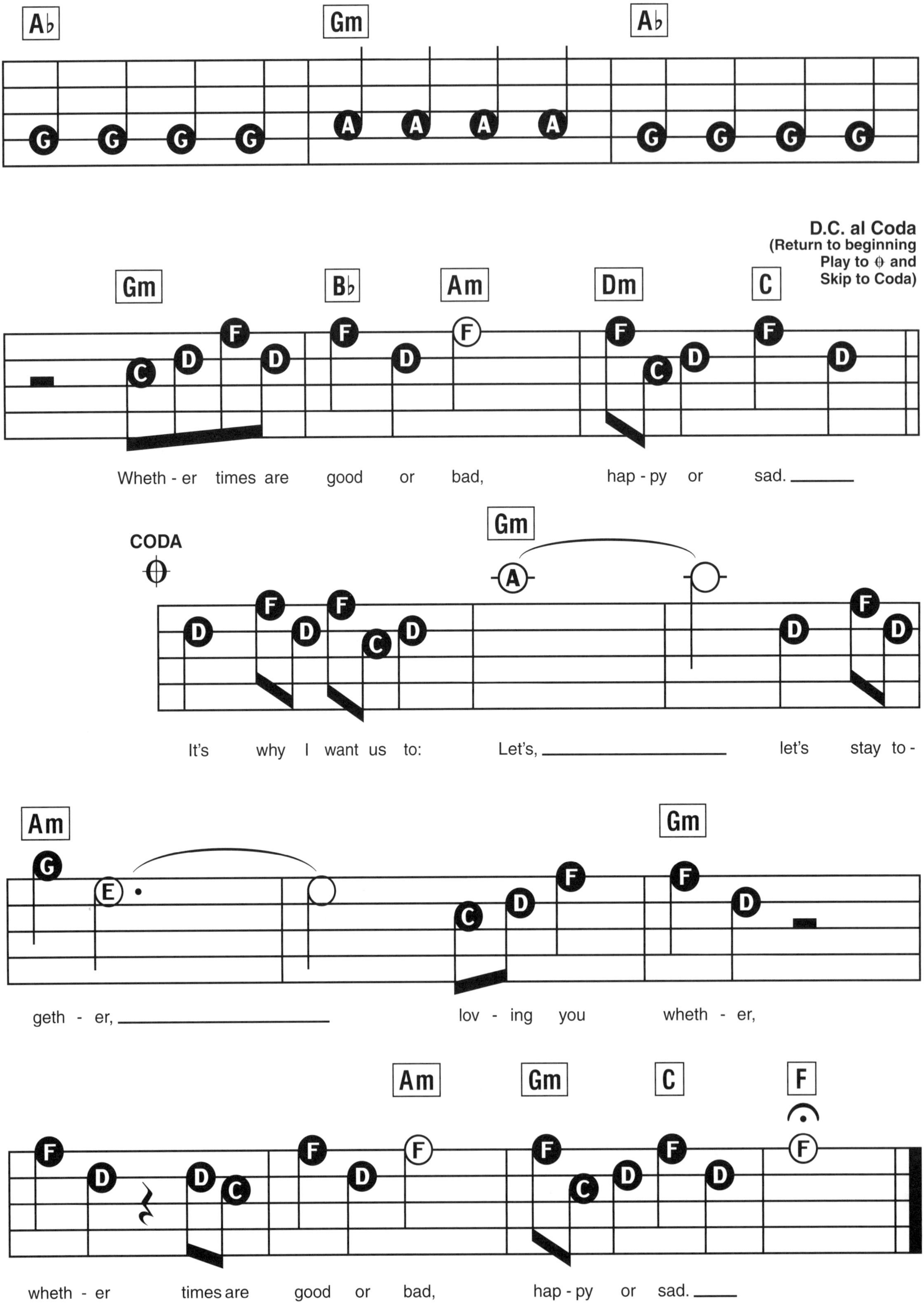
A♭ Gm A♭
D.C. al Coda
(Return to beginning
Play to ⊕ and
Skip to Coda)
Gm B♭ Am Dm C
Wheth - er times are good or bad, hap - py or sad.
CODA
Gm
It's why I want us to: Let's, let's stay to -
Am Gm
geth - er, lov - ing you wheth - er,
Am Gm C F
wheth - er times are good or bad, hap - py or sad.

More Than Words

Registration 2
Rhythm: Reggae or Rock

Words and Music by Nuno Bettencourt
and Gary Cherone

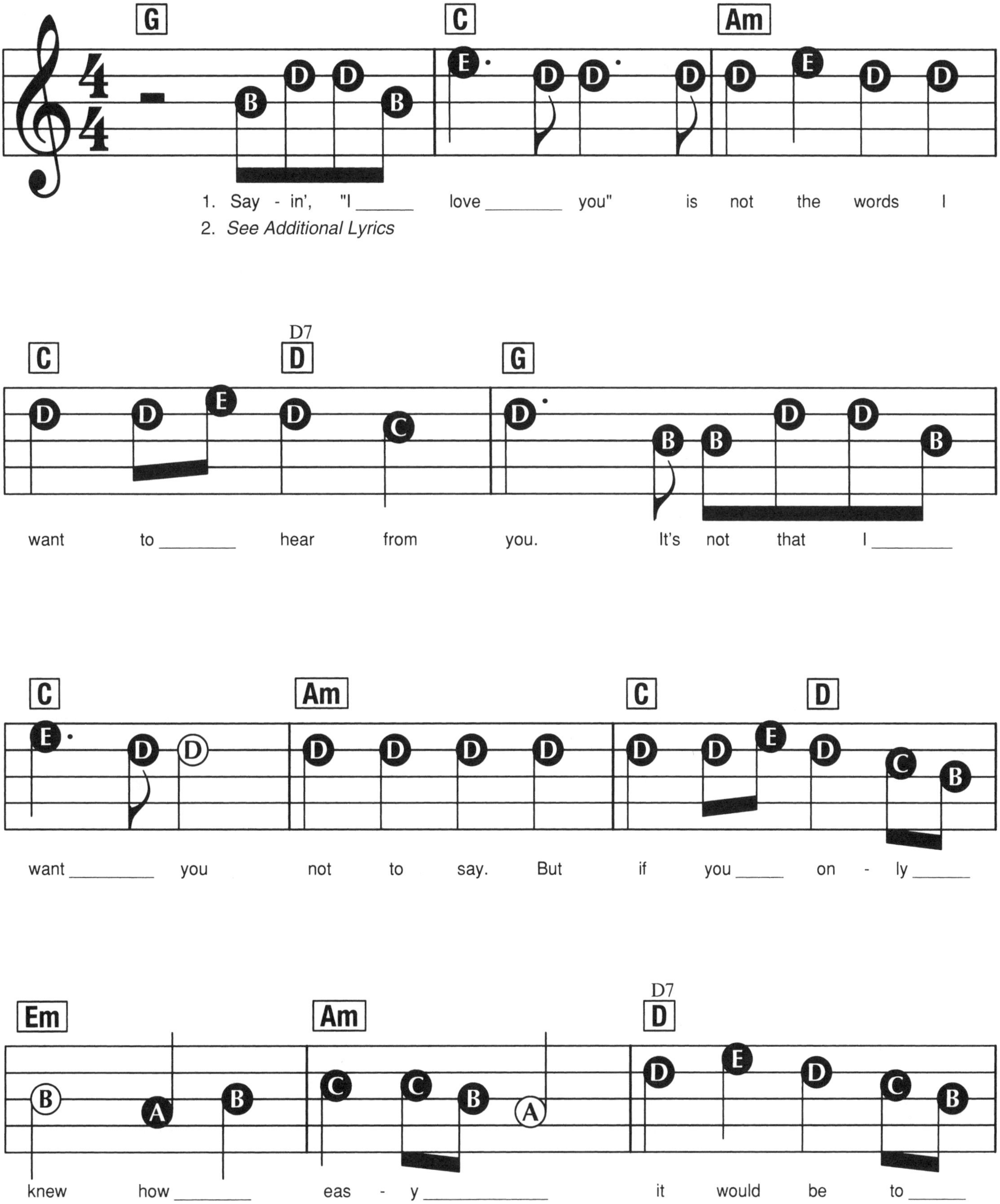
G C Am
1. Say - in', "I ___ love ___ you" is not the words I
2. *See Additional Lyrics*
C D7 D G
want to ___ hear from you. It's not that I ___
C Am C D
want ___ you not to say. But if you ___ on - ly ___
Em Am D7 D
knew how ___ eas - y ___ it would be to ___

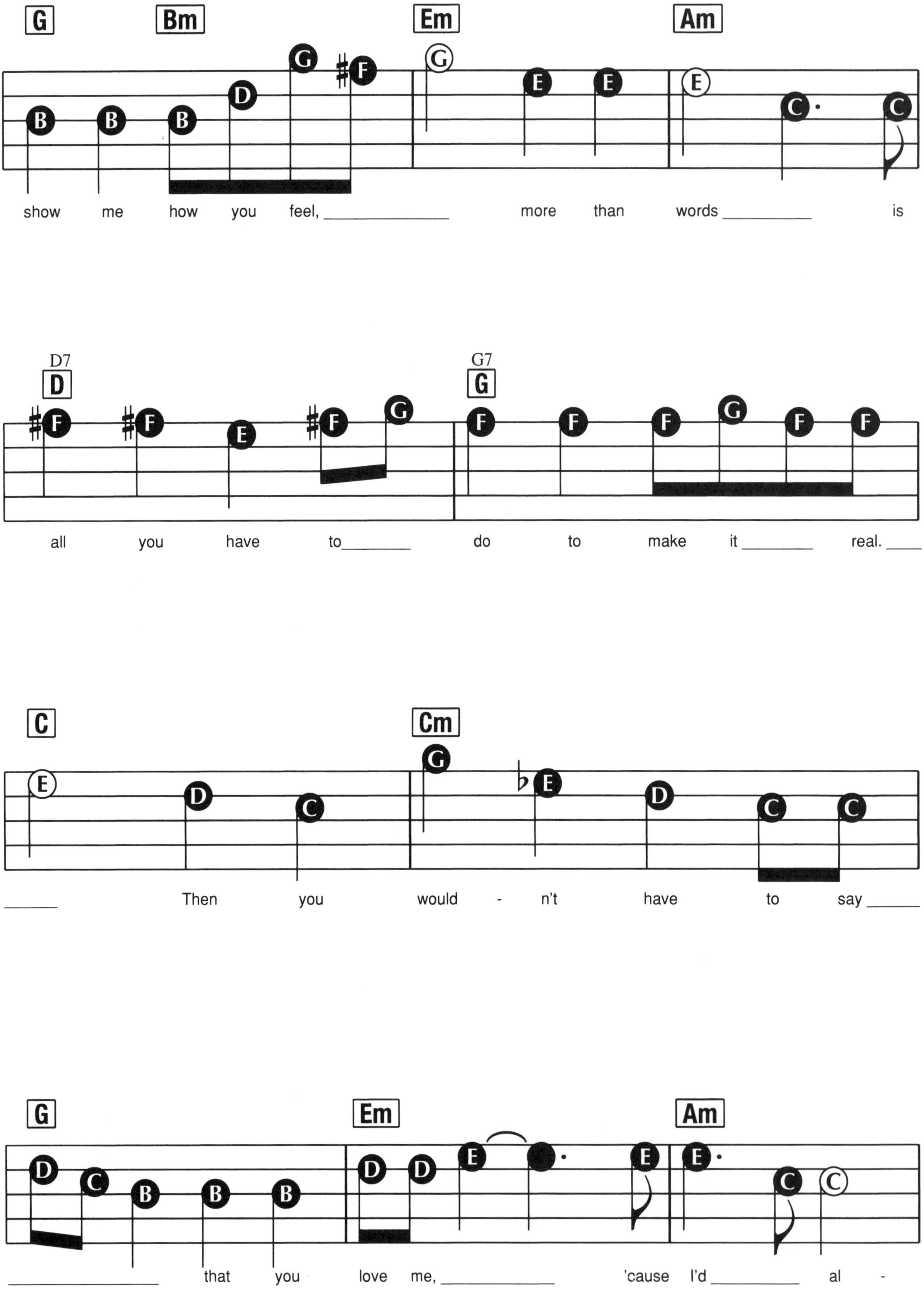
G Bm Em Am
B B B D G ♯F G E E E C C
show me how you feel, more than words is
D7 D G7 G
♯F ♯F E ♯F G F F F G F F
all you have to do to make it real.
C Cm
E D C G ♭E D C C
Then you would - n't have to say
G Em Am
D C B B B D D E E E E C C
that you love me, 'cause I'd al -

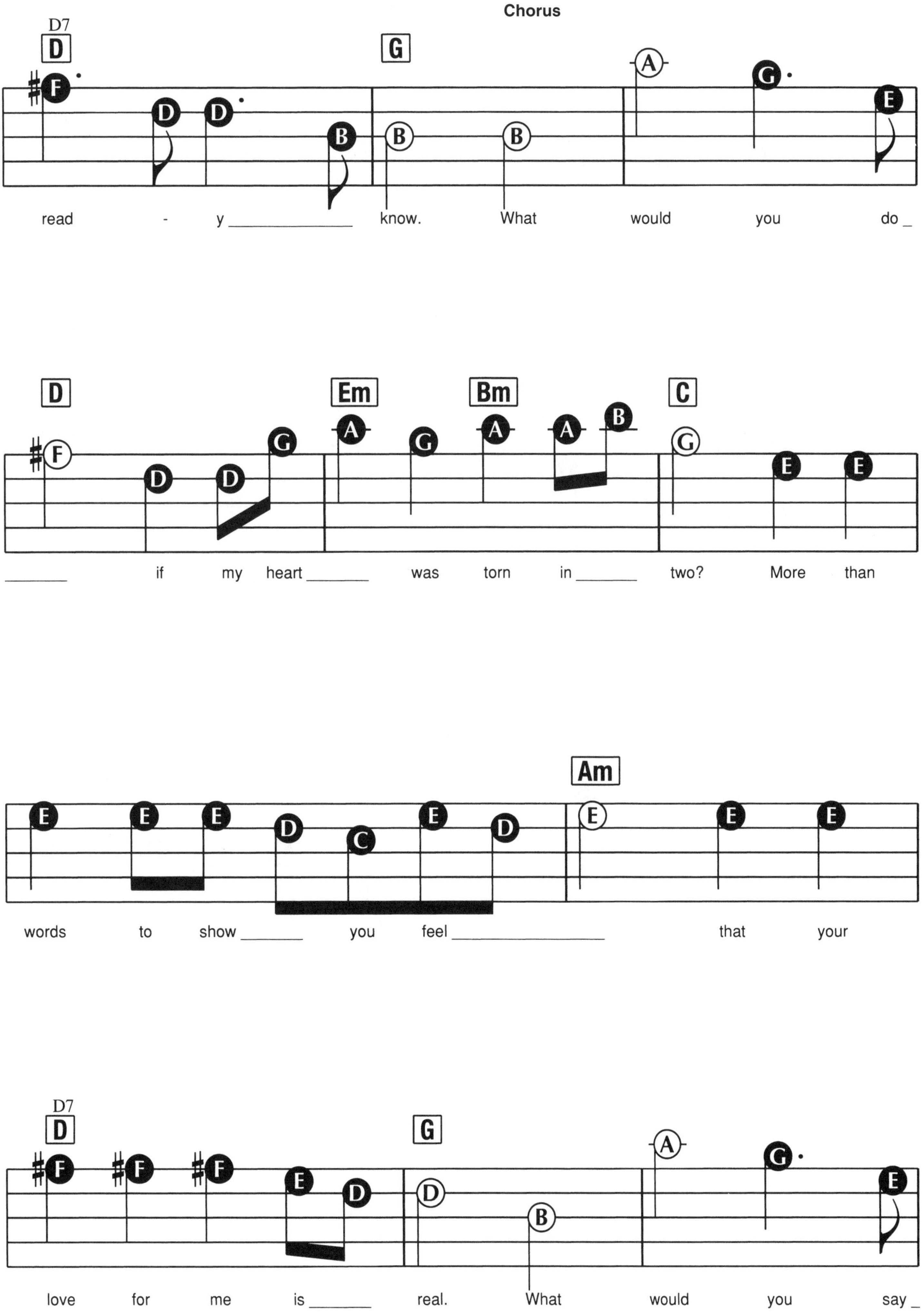
Chorus
D7 D G
read - y ___ know. What would you do _
D Em Bm C
___ if my heart ___ was torn in ___ two? More than
Am
words to show ___ you feel ___ that your
D7 D G
love for me is ___ real. What would you say _

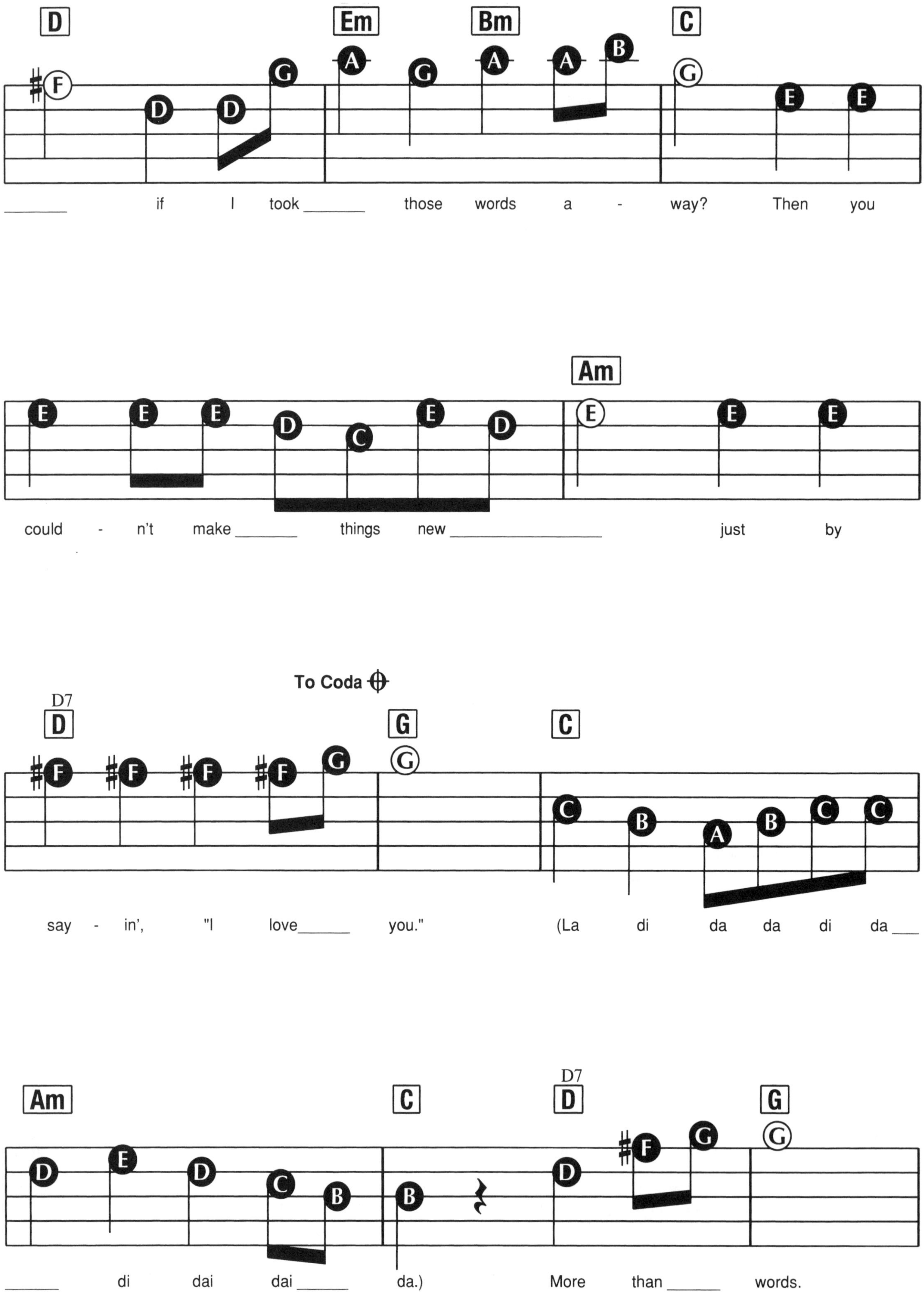
D Em Bm C
if I took those words a - way? Then you
Am
could - n't make things new just by
To Coda
D7
D G C
say - in', "I love you." (La di da da di da
Am C D7 D G
di dai dai da.) More than words.

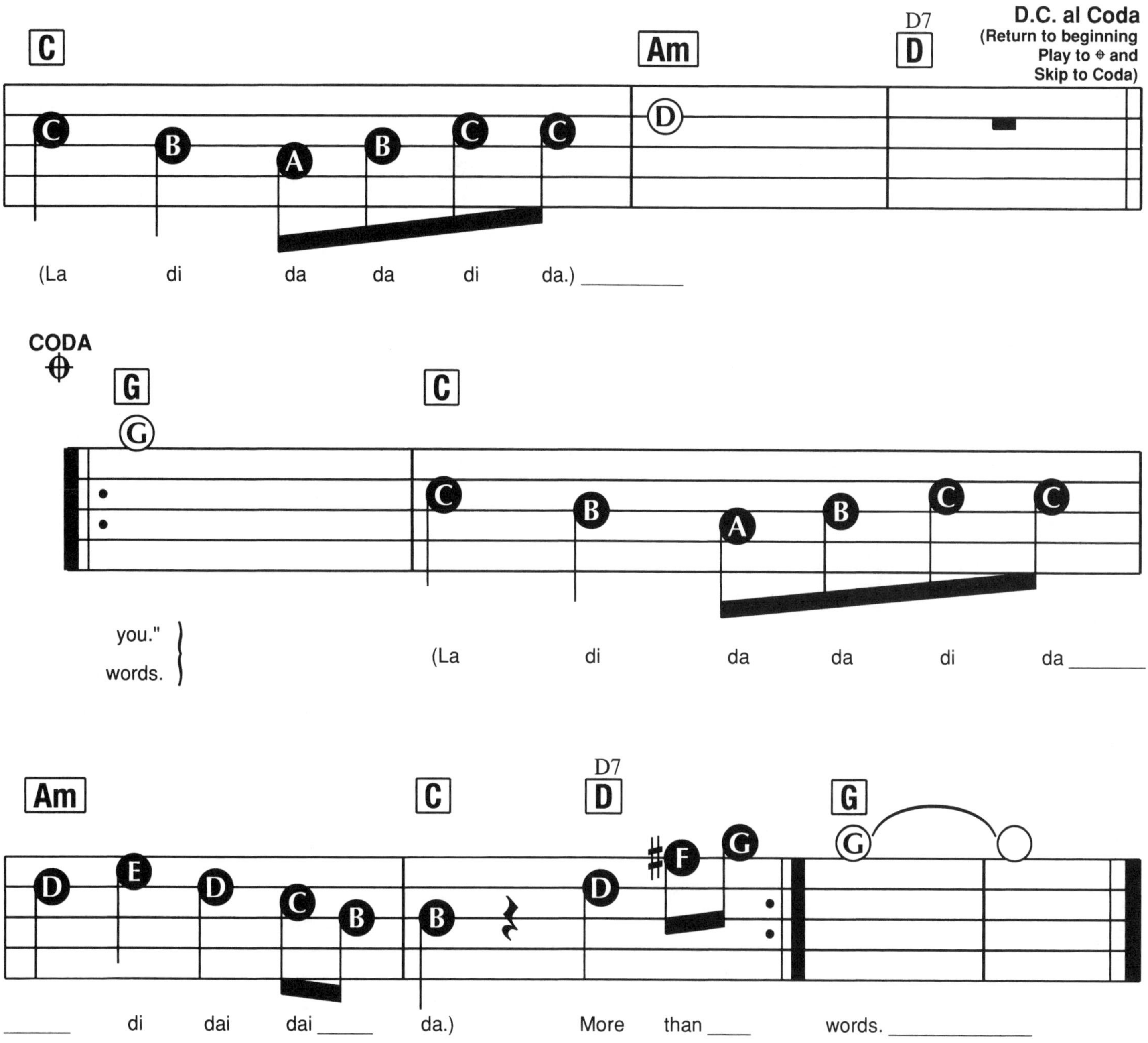

Additional Lyrics

2. Now that I have tried to talk to you
And make you understand.
All you have to do is close your eyes
And just reach out your hands.
And touch me, hold me close, don't ever let me go.
More than words is all I ever needed you to show.
Then you wouldn't have to say
That you love me 'cause I'd already know.

Chorus

Look for the Silver Lining
from SALLY

Registration 2
Rhythm: Fox Trot or Swing

Words by Buddy DeSylva
Music by Jerome Kern

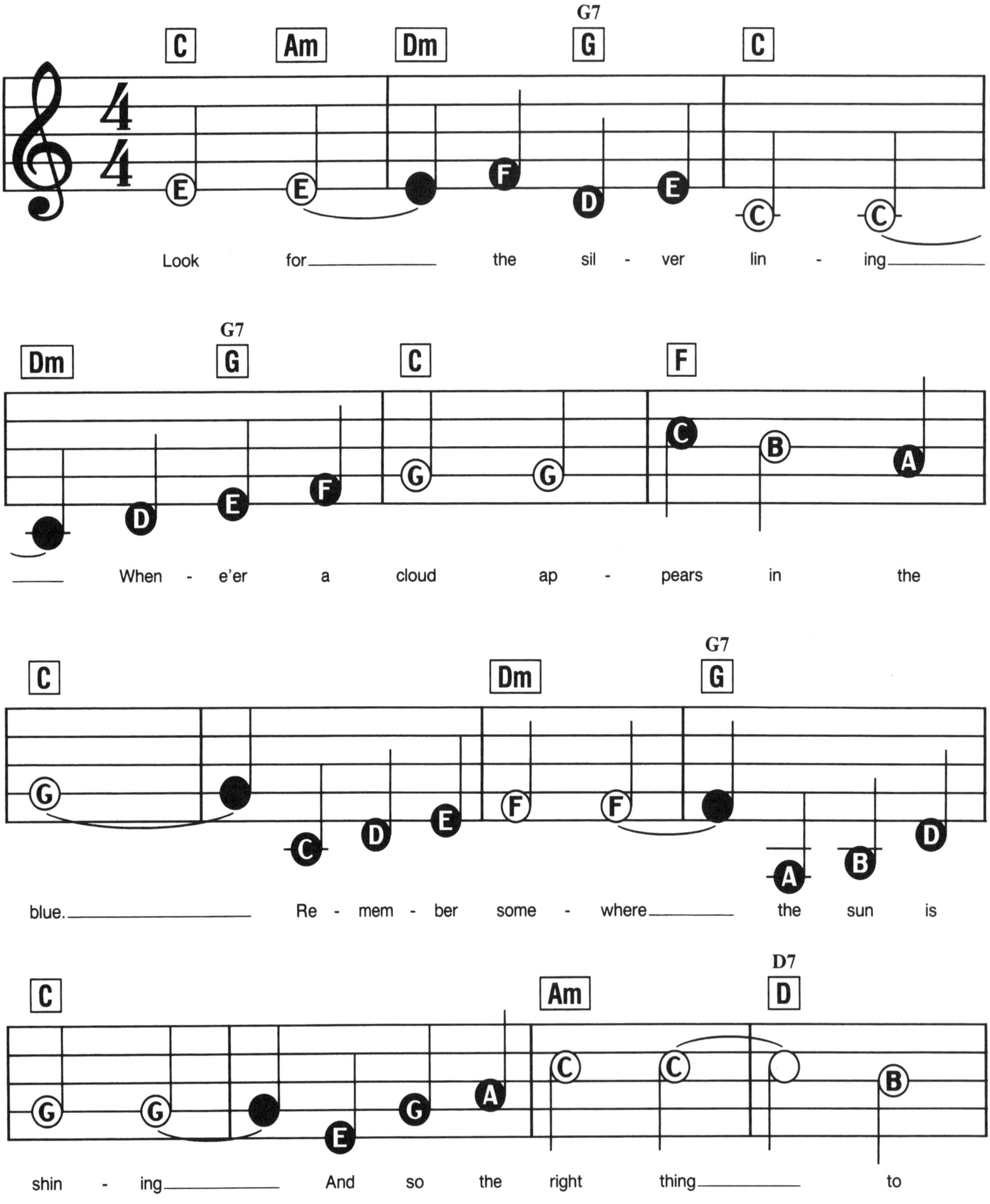
C Am Dm G7 G C
Look for the sil - ver lin - ing
Dm G7 G C F
When - e'er a cloud ap - pears in the
C Dm G7 G
blue. Re - mem - ber some - where the sun is
C Am D7 D
shin - ing And so the right thing to

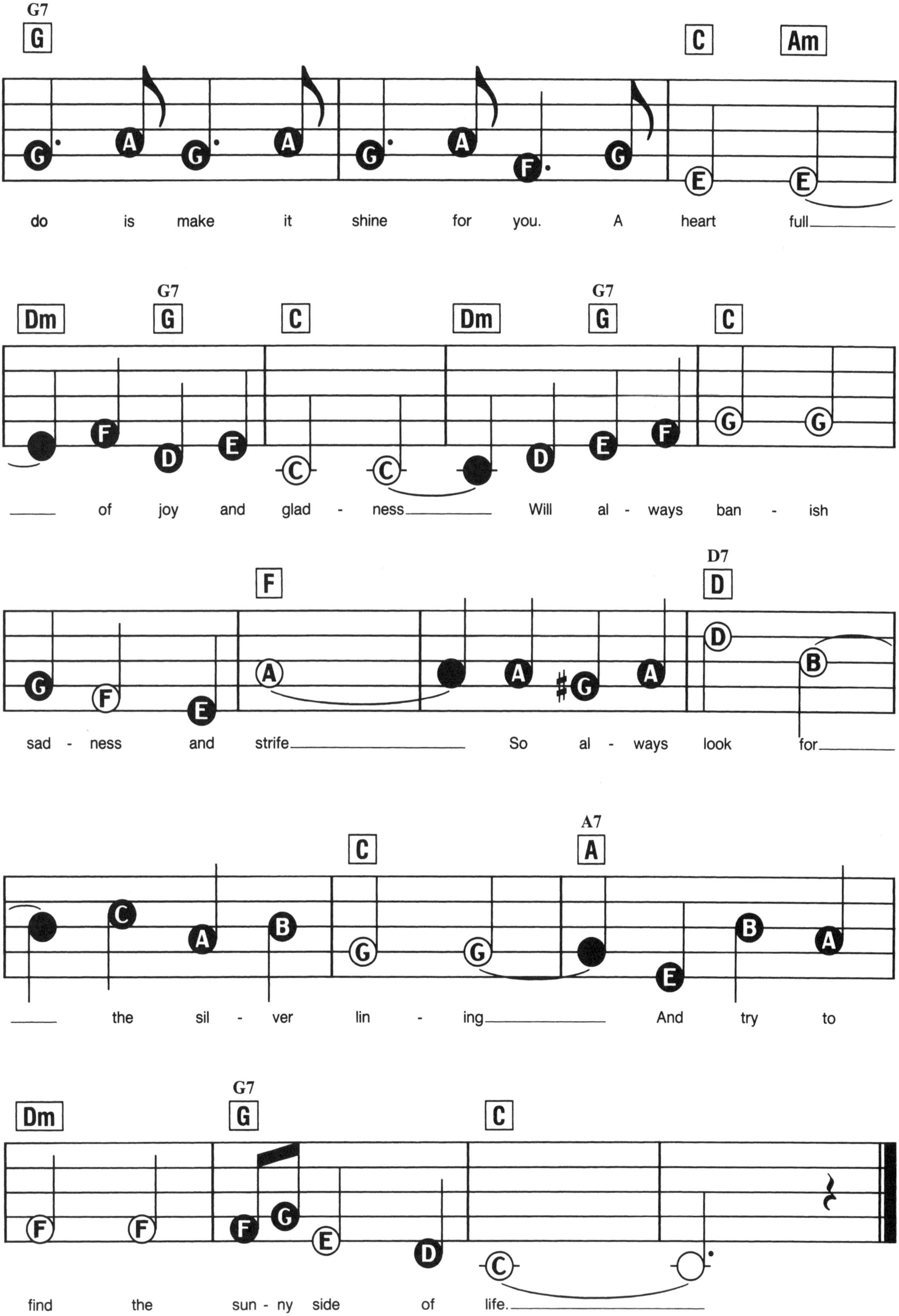
G7 G C Am
do is make it shine for you. A heart full
Dm G7 G C Dm G7 G C
of joy and glad - ness Will al - ways ban - ish
F D7 D
sad - ness and strife So al - ways look for
C A7 A
the sil - ver lin - ing And try to
Dm G7 G C
find the sun - ny side of life.

Lovely to Look At

from ROBERTA

Registration 4
Rhythm: Ballad or Swing

Words and Music by Jimmy McHugh,
Dorothy Fields and Jerome Kern

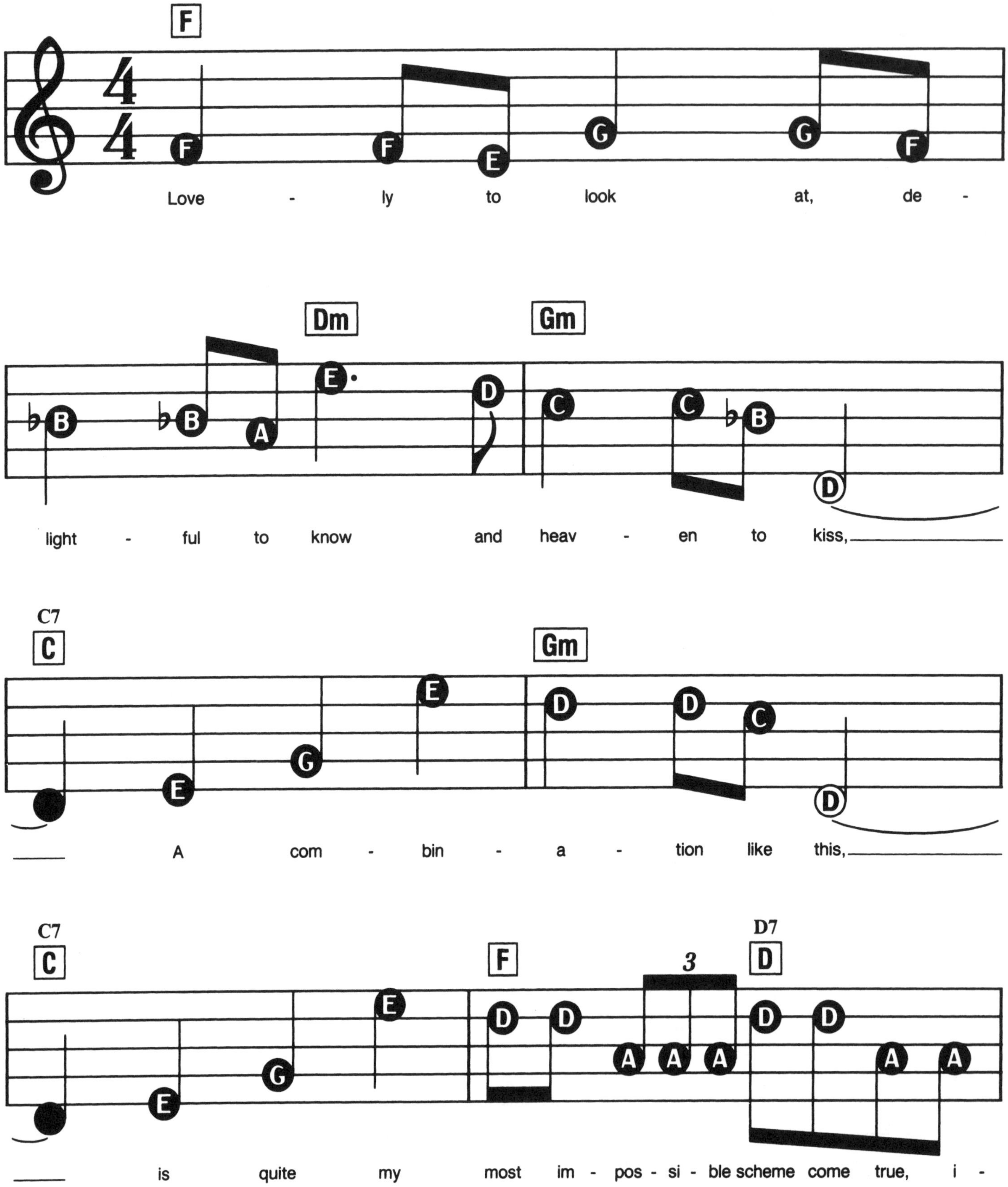
F
Love - ly to look at, de -
Dm Gm
light - ful to know and heav - en to kiss,
C7 C Gm
A com - bin - a - tion like this,
C7 C F D7 D
is quite my most im - pos - si - ble scheme come true, i -

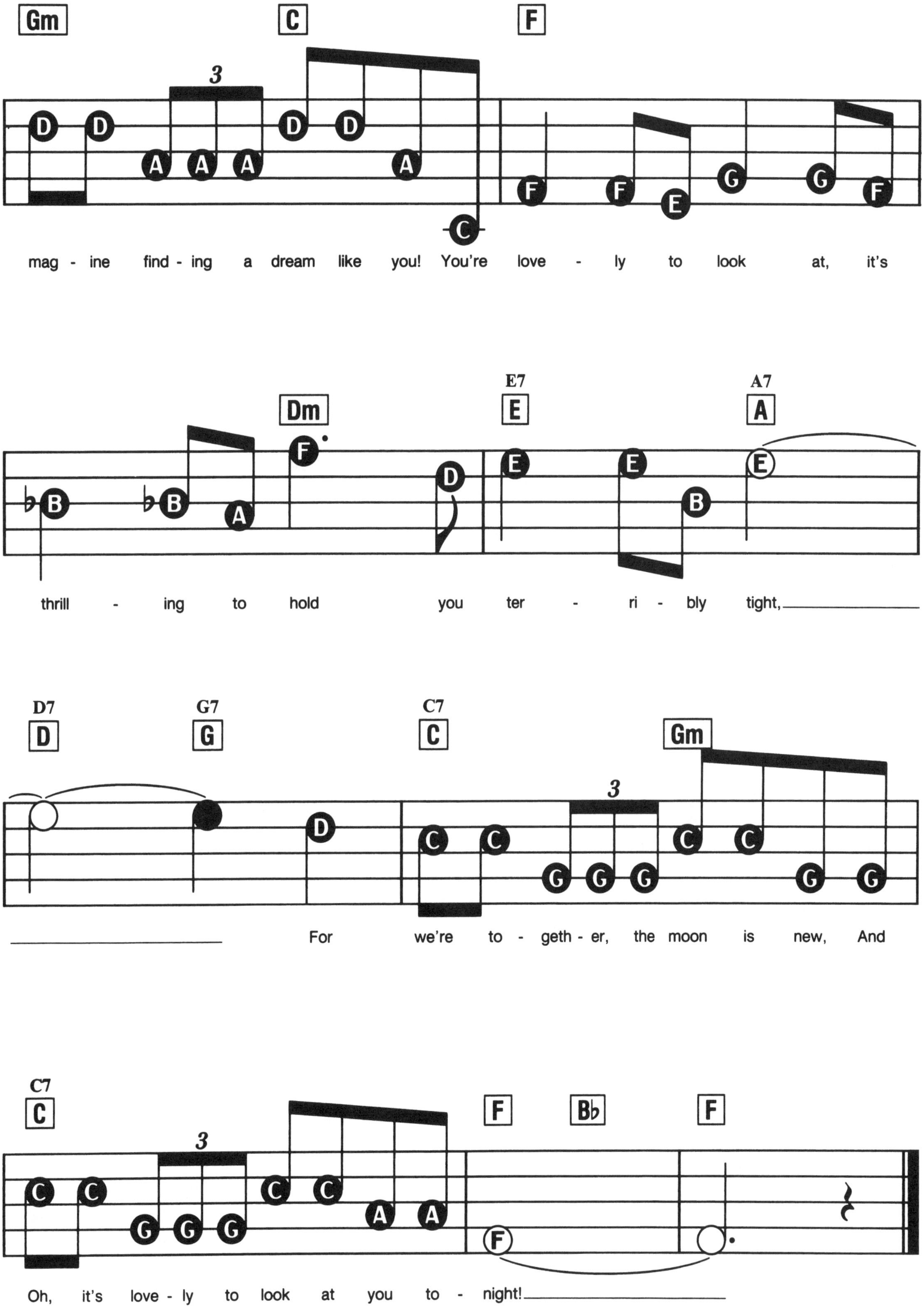
Gm C F
mag - ine find - ing a dream like you! You're love - ly to look at, it's
Dm E7 E A7 A
thrill - ing to hold you ter - ri - bly tight,
D7 D G7 G C7 C Gm
For we're to - geth - er, the moon is new, And
C7 C F B♭ F
Oh, it's love - ly to look at you to - night!

Make Believe

from SHOW BOAT

Registration 10
Rhythm: Ballad or Fox Trot

Lyrics by Oscar Hammerstein II
Music by Jerome Kern

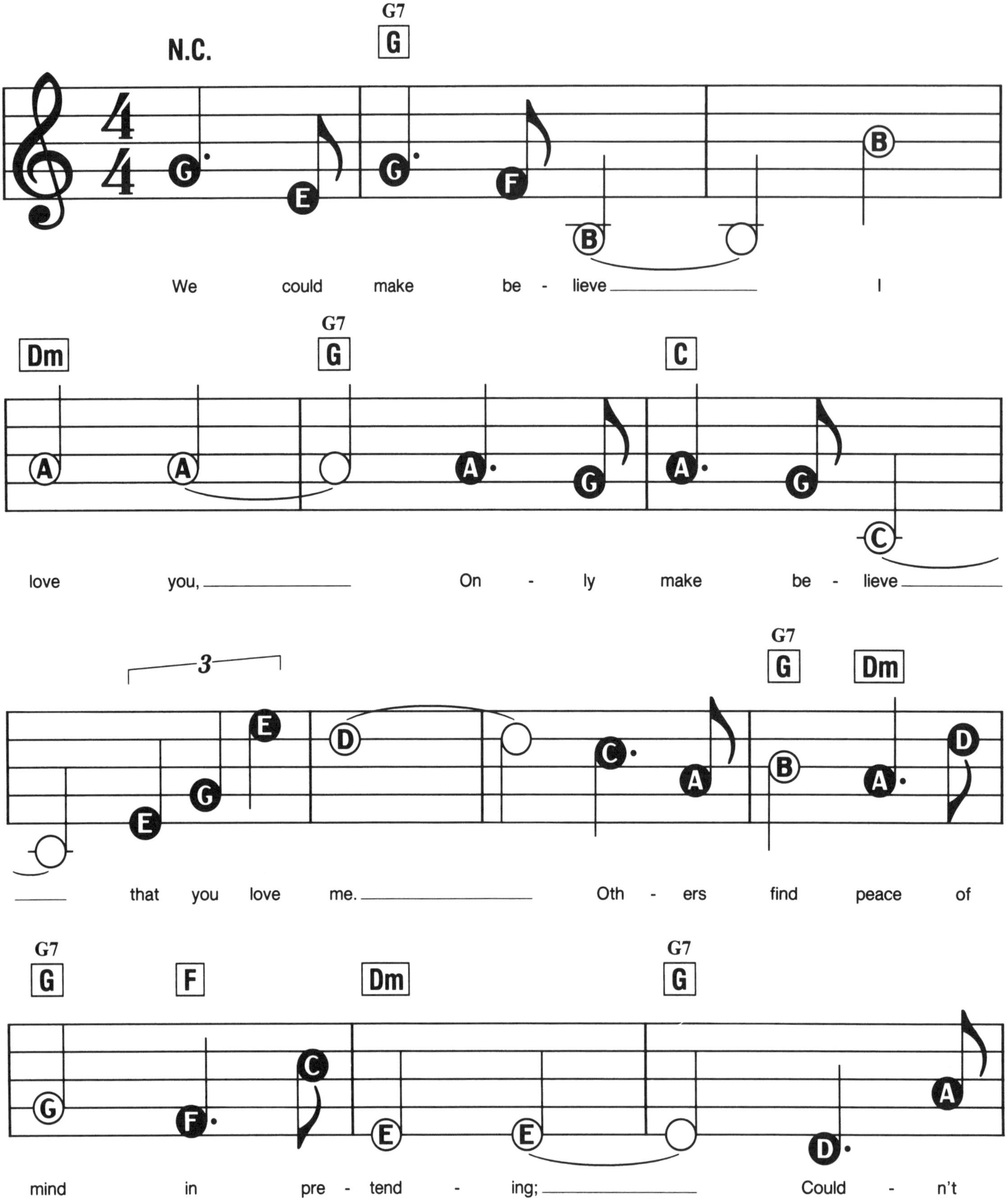
N.C.
G7
We could make be - lieve I
Dm G7 C
love you, On - ly make be - lieve
3
that you love me. Oth - ers find peace of
G7 Dm
G7 F Dm G7
mind in pre - tend - ing; Could - n't

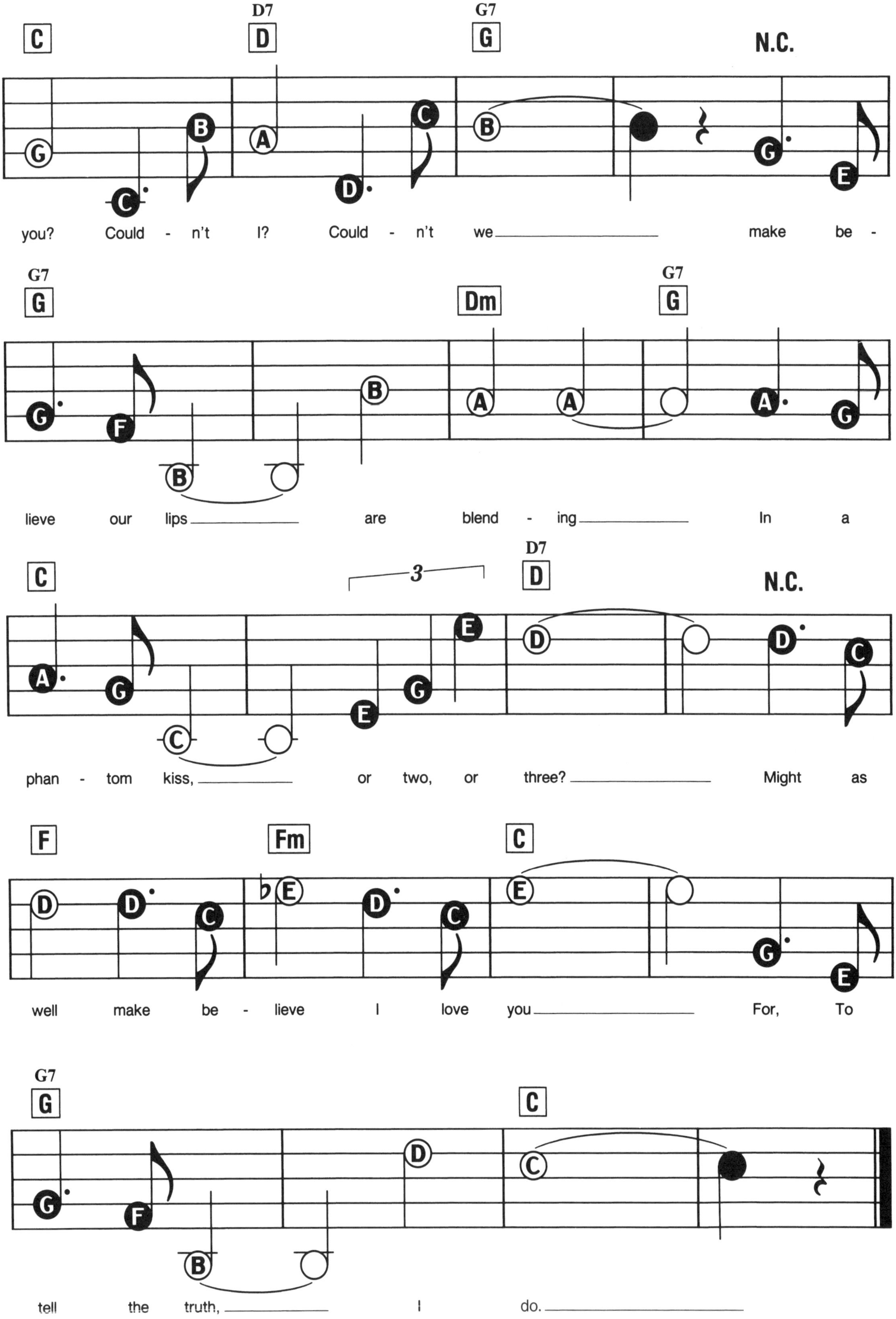
C D7 D G7 G N.C.
you? Could - n't I? Could - n't we make be -
G7 G Dm G7 G
lieve our lips are blend - ing In a
C 3 D7 D N.C.
phan - tom kiss, or two, or three? Might as
F Fm C
well make be - lieve I love you For, To
G7 G C
tell the truth, I do.

My Romance

from JUMBO

Registration 5
Rhythm: Fox Trot or Ballad

Words by Lorenz Hart
Music by Richard Rodgers

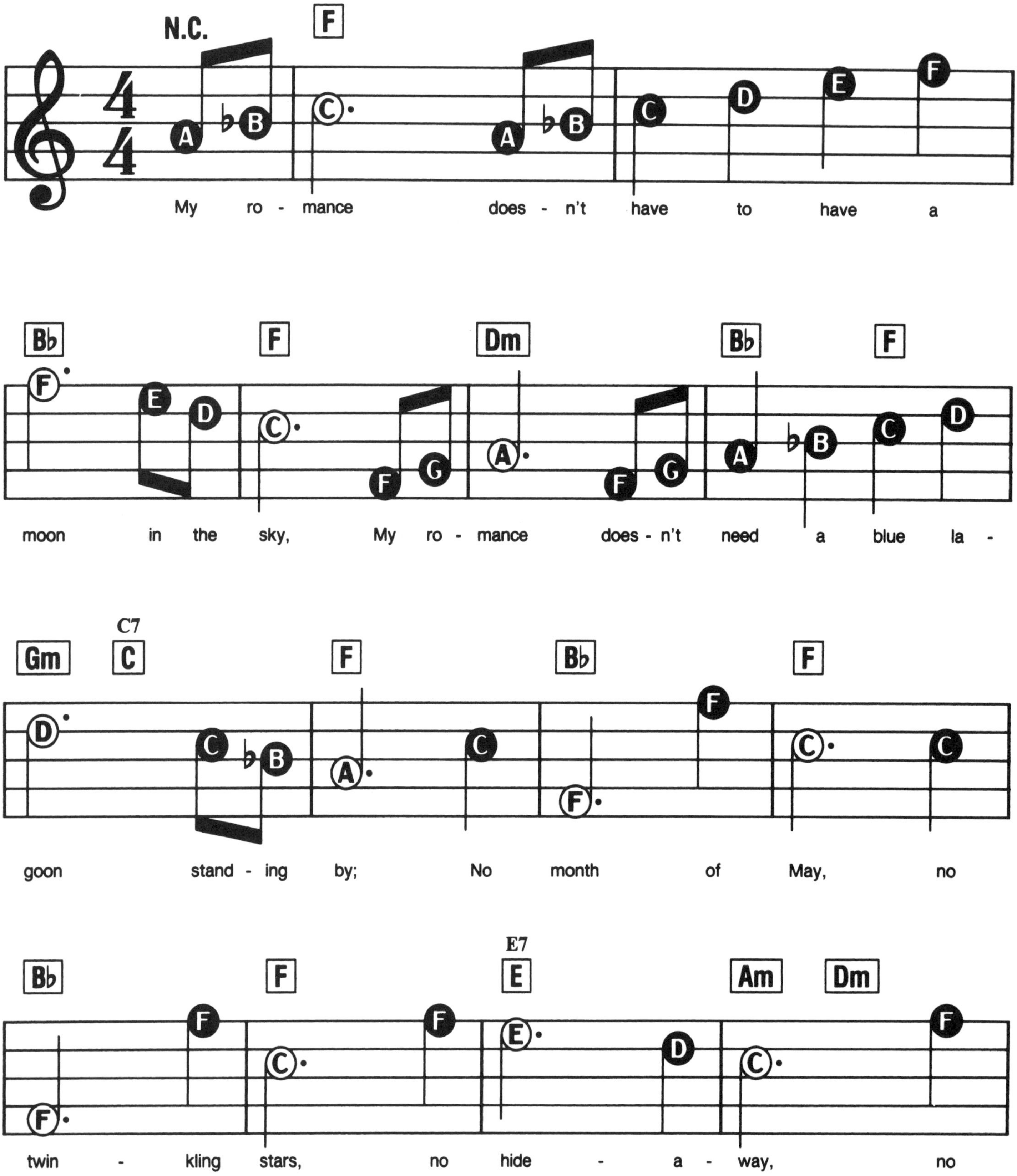
N.C.
F
My ro - mance does - n't have to have a
B♭ F Dm B♭ F
moon in the sky, My ro - mance does - n't need a blue la -
Gm C7 C F B♭ F
goon stand - ing by; No month of May, no
B♭ F E7 E Am Dm
twin - kling stars, no hide - a - way, no

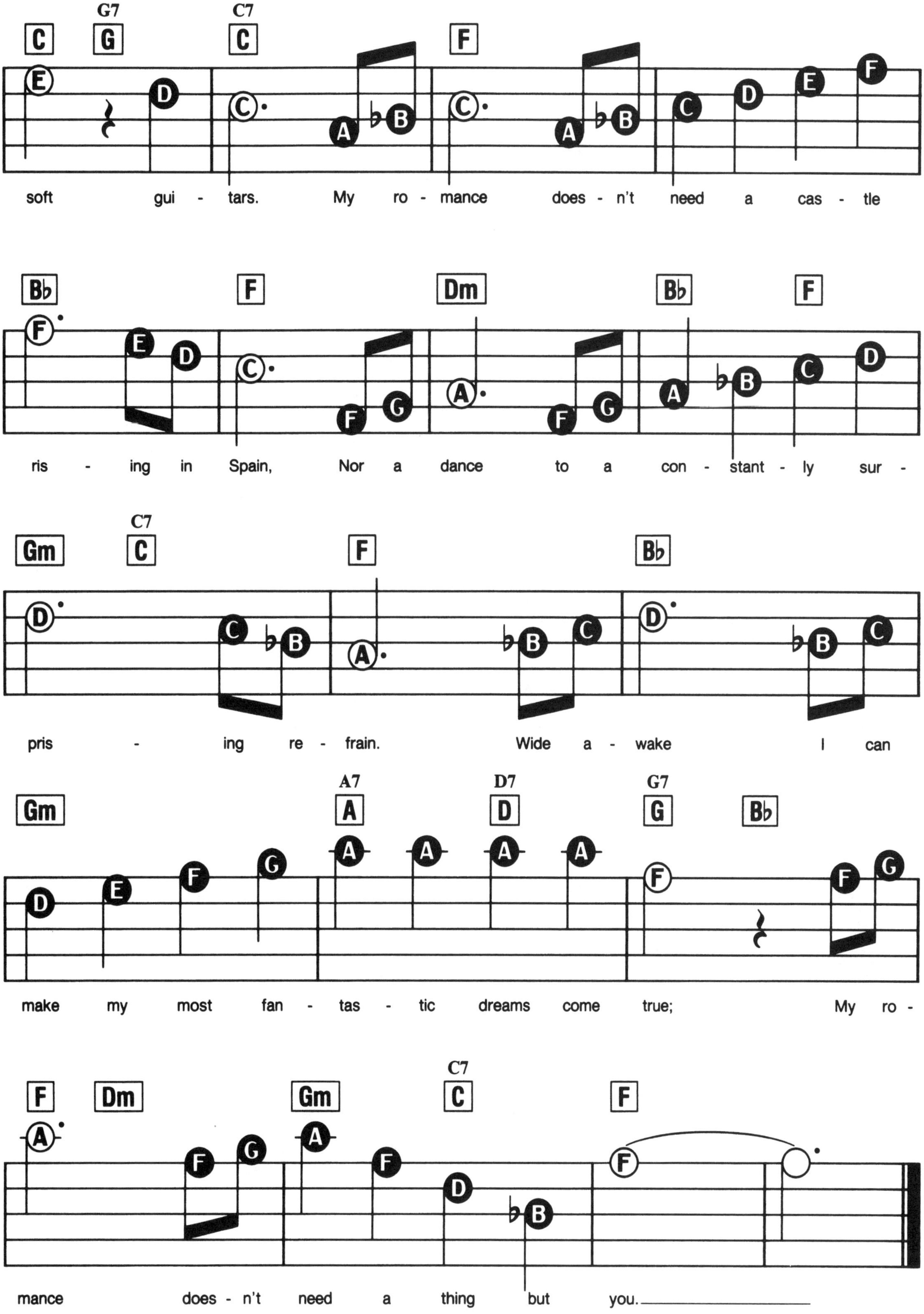
C G7 G C7 C F
soft gui - tars. My ro - mance does - n't need a cas - tle
B♭ F Dm B♭ F
ris - ing in Spain, Nor a dance to a con - stant - ly sur -
Gm C7 C F B♭
pris - ing re - frain. Wide a - wake I can
Gm A7 A D7 D G7 G B♭
make my most fan - tas - tic dreams come true; My ro -
F Dm Gm C7 C F
mance does - n't need a thing but you.

They Didn't Believe Me

from THE GIRL FROM UTAH

Registration 2
Rhythm: Ballad or Swing

Words by Herbert Reynolds
Music by Jerome Kern

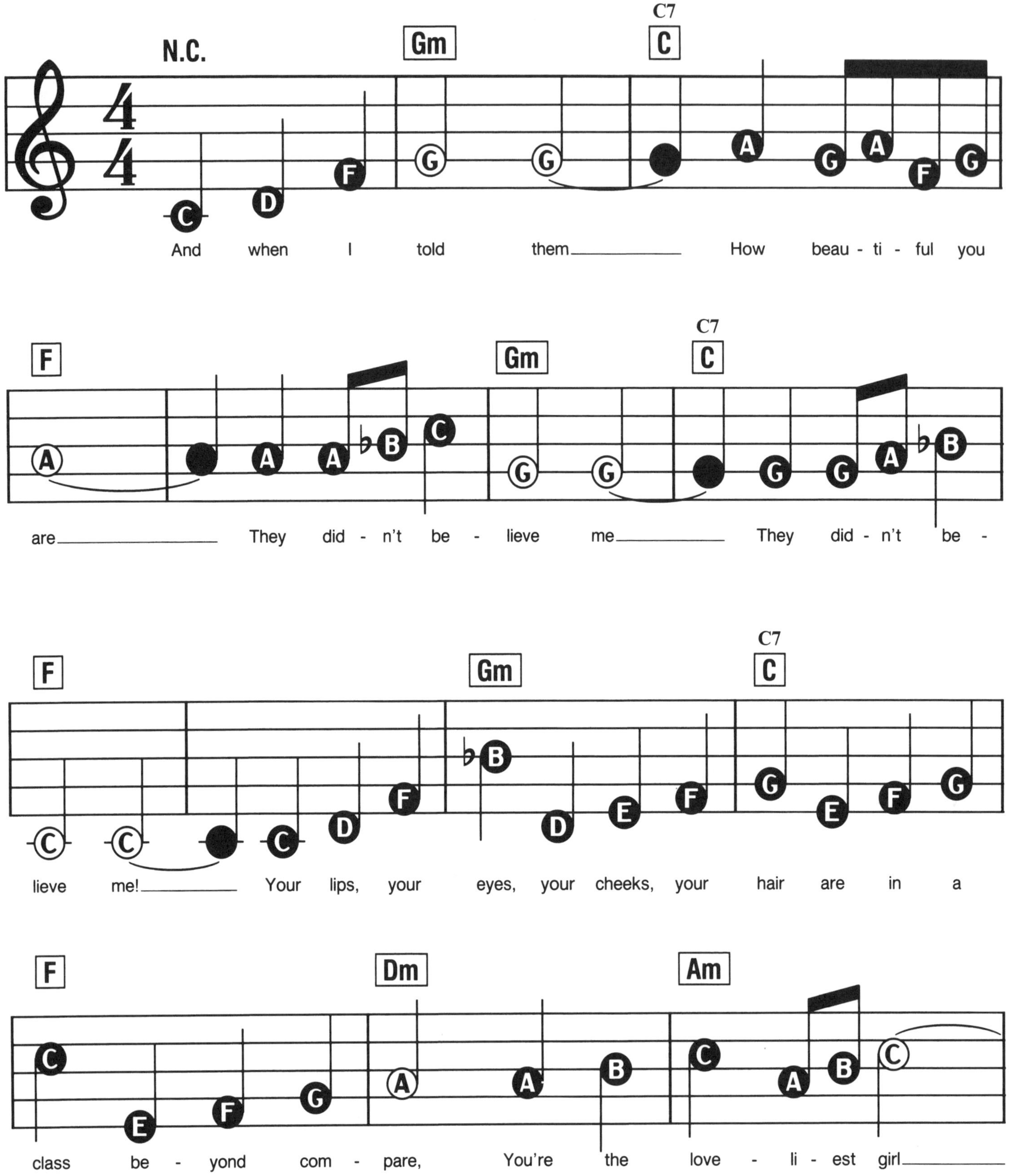
N.C.
Gm
C7
C
And when I told them How beau - ti - ful you
F
Gm
C7
C
are They did - n't be - lieve me They did - n't be -
F
Gm
C7
C
lieve me! Your lips, your eyes, your cheeks, your hair are in a
F
Dm
Am
class be - yond com - pare, You're the love - li - est girl

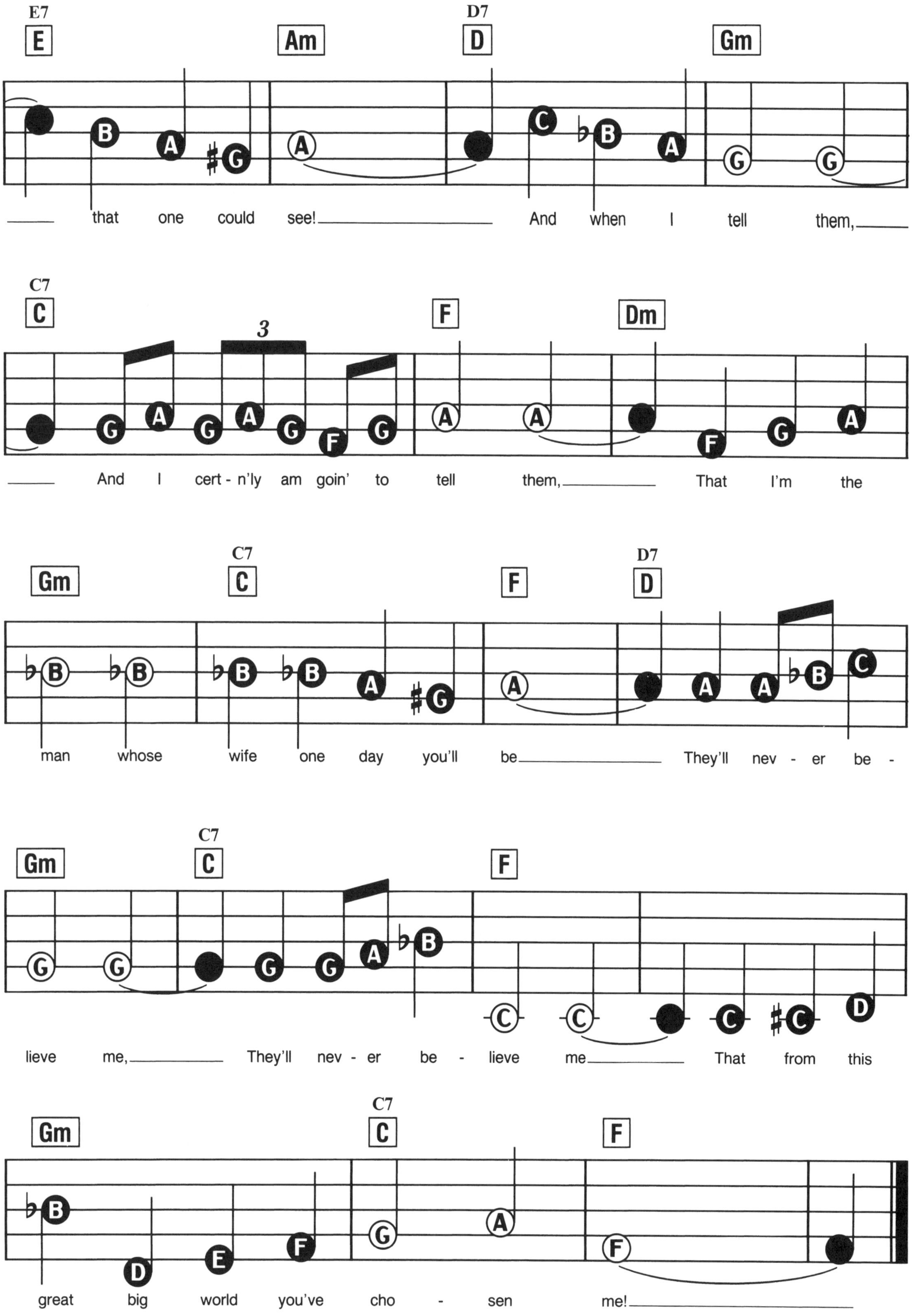
E7 E Am D7 D Gm
that one could see! And when I tell them,
C7 C 3 F Dm
And I cert - n'ly am goin' to tell them, That I'm the
Gm C7 C F D7 D
man whose wife one day you'll be They'll nev - er be -
Gm C7 C F
lieve me, They'll nev - er be - lieve me That from this
Gm C7 C F
great big world you've cho - sen me!

Why Do I Love You?
from SHOW BOAT

Registration 3
Rhythm: Fox Trot or Swing

Lyrics by Oscar Hammerstein II
Music by Jerome Kern

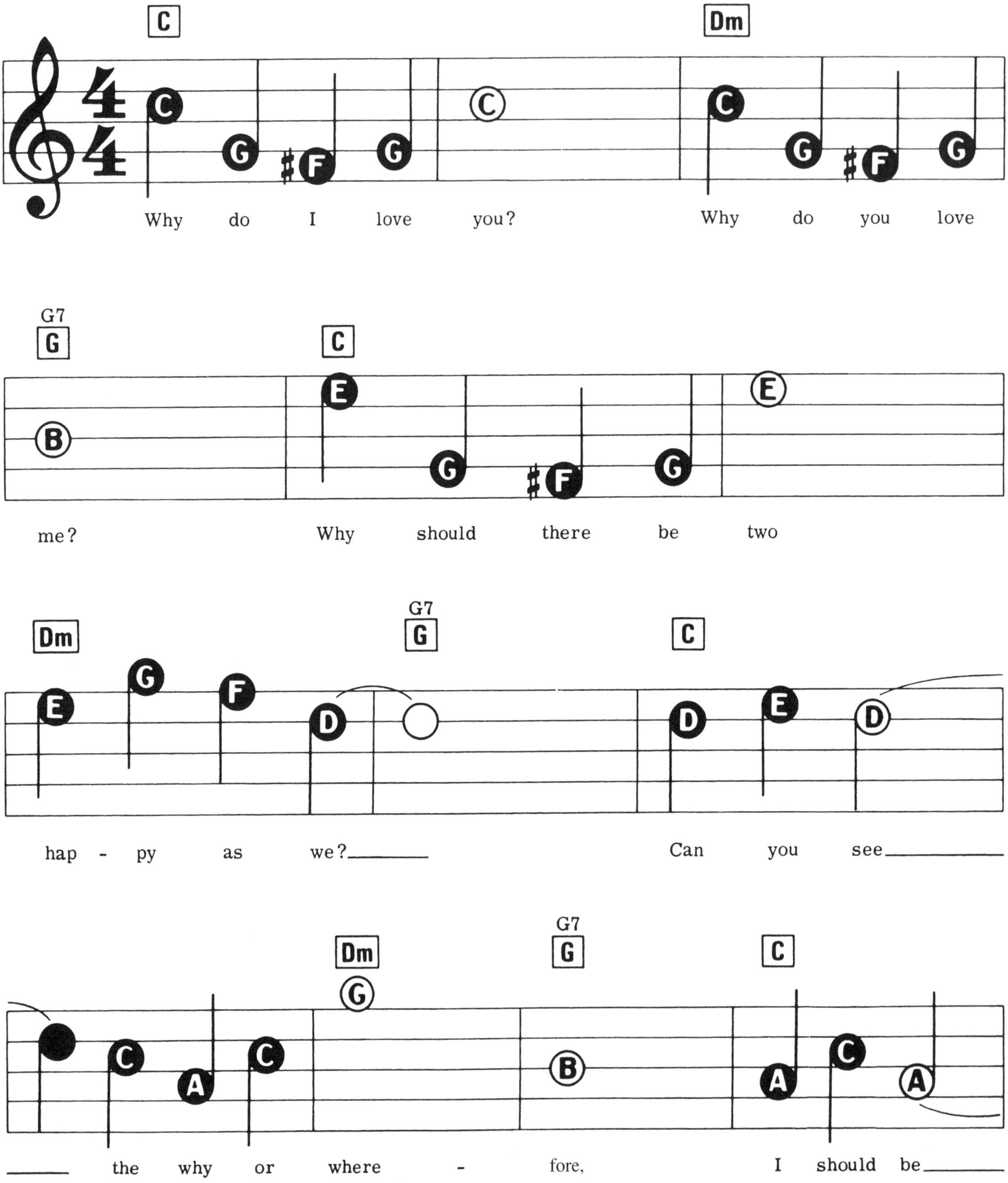
C
Dm
Why do I love you? Why do you love
G7
G
C
me? Why should there be two
Dm
G7
G
C
hap - py as we? Can you see
Dm
G7
G
C
the why or where - fore, I should be

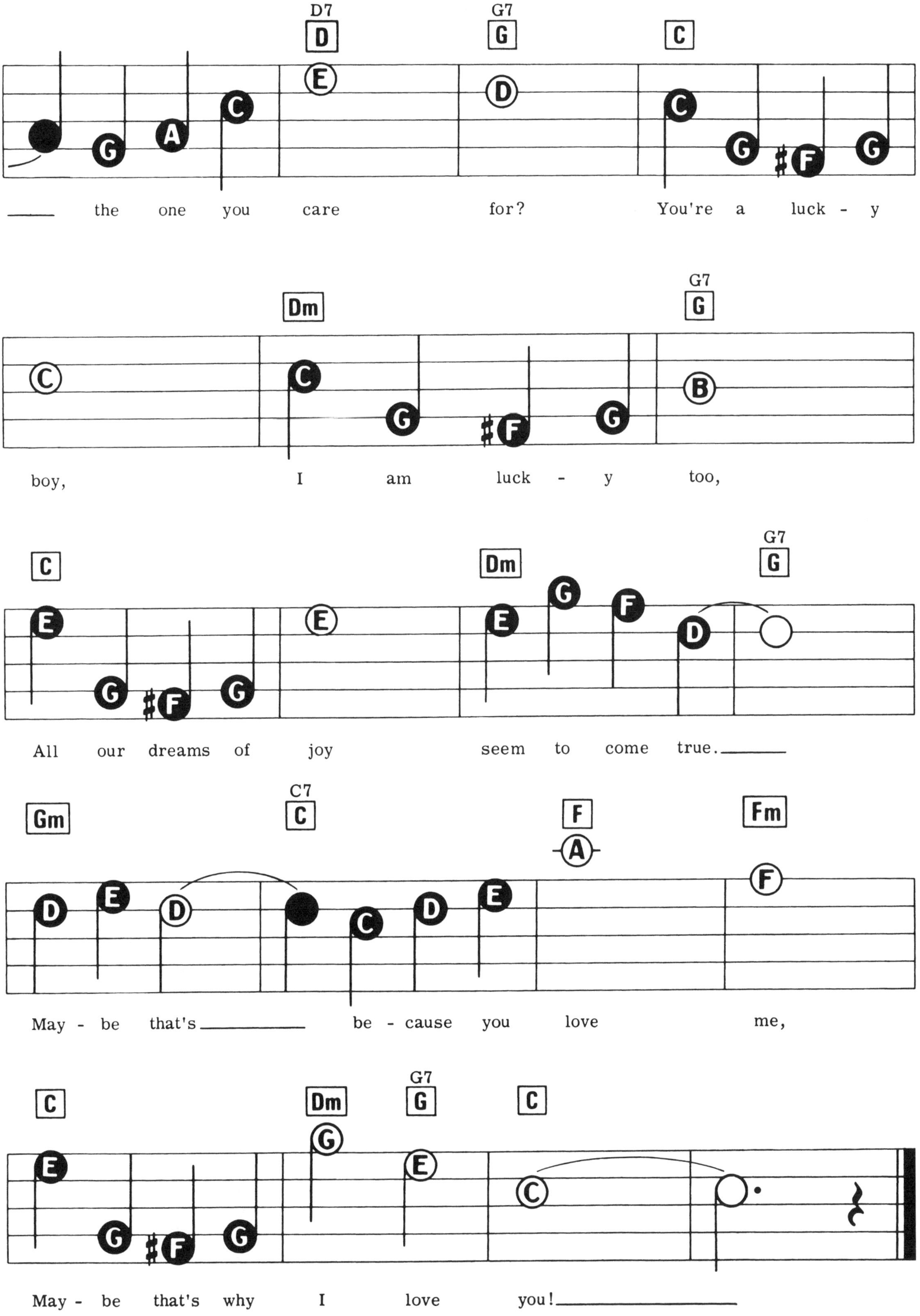
D7 D G7 G C
the one you care for? You're a luck - y
Dm G7 G
boy, I am luck - y too,
C Dm G7 G
All our dreams of joy seem to come true.
Gm C7 C F Fm
May - be that's be - cause you love me,
C Dm G7 G C
May - be that's why I love you!

You Are Too Beautiful

from HALLELUJAH, I'M A BUM

Registration 10
Rhythm: Swing

Words by Lorenz Hart
Music by Richard Rodgers

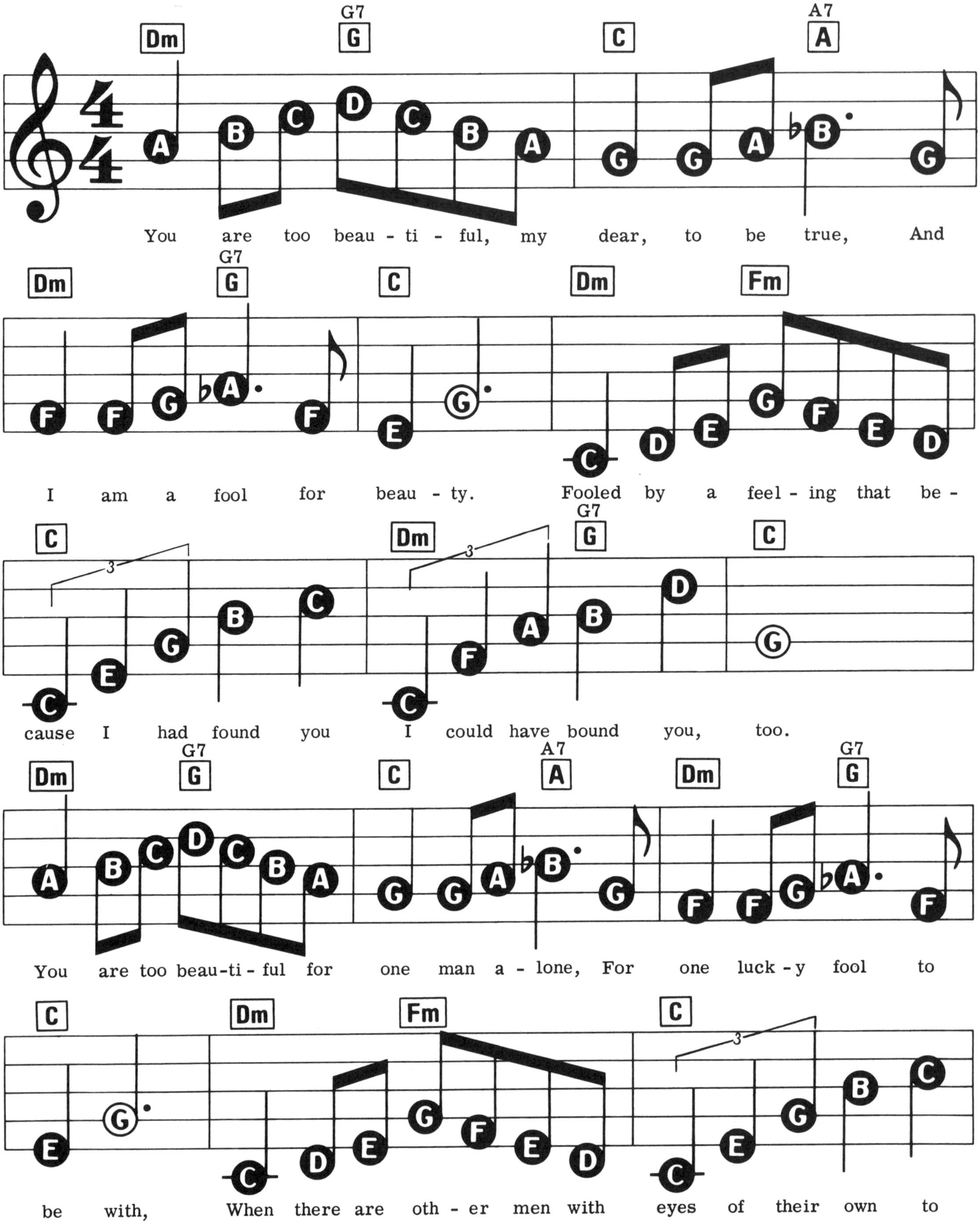
You are too beau - ti - ful, my dear, to be true, And
I am a fool for beau - ty. Fooled by a feel - ing that be -
cause I had found you I could have bound you, too.
You are too beau-ti - ful for one man a - lone, For one luck - y fool to
be with, When there are oth - er men with eyes of their own to

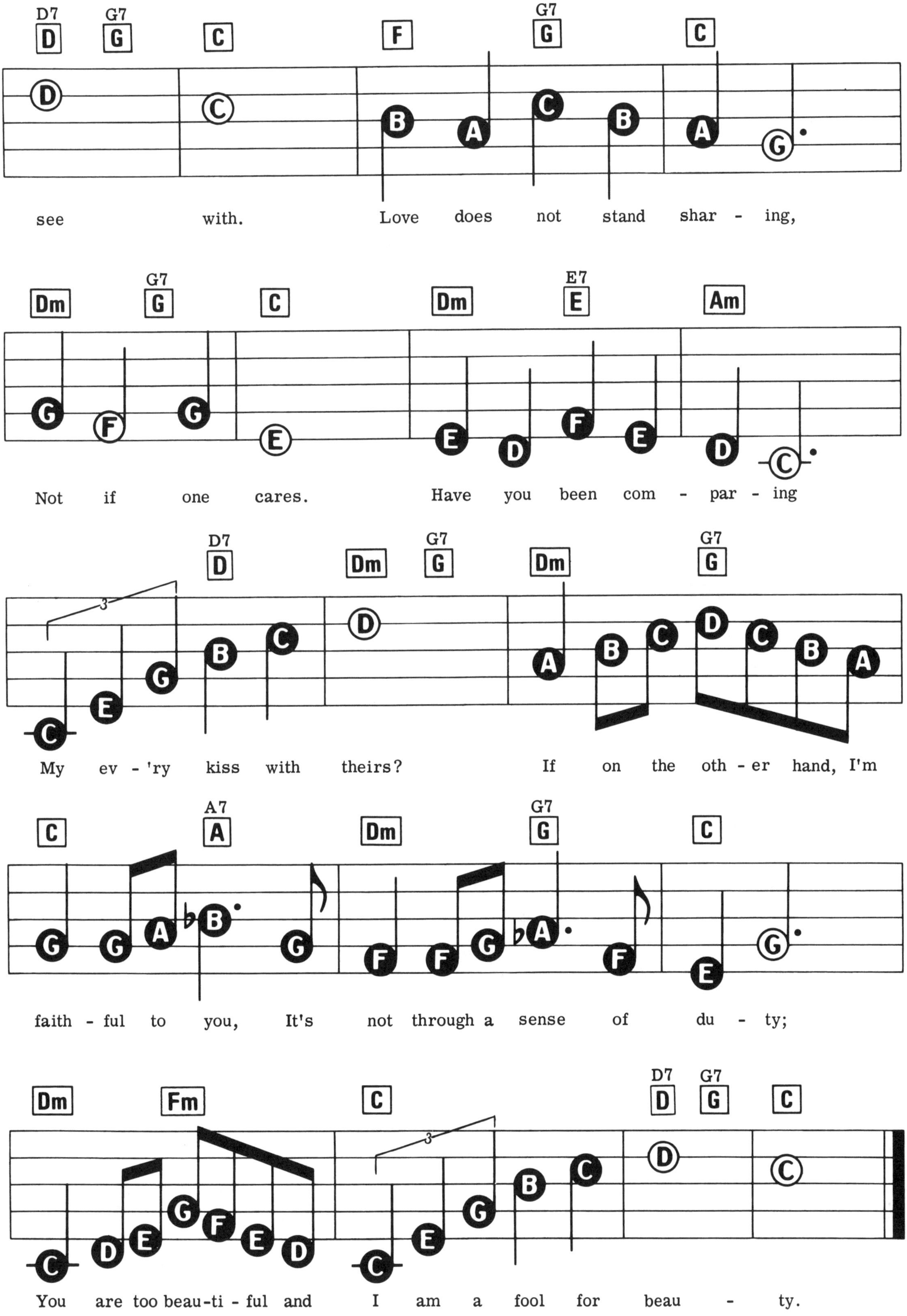
D7 D G7 G C F G7 G C
see with. Love does not stand shar - ing,
Dm G7 G C Dm E7 E Am
Not if one cares. Have you been com - par - ing
D7 D Dm G7 G Dm G7 G
My ev - 'ry kiss with theirs? If on the oth - er hand, I'm
C A7 A Dm G7 G C
faith - ful to you, It's not through a sense of du - ty;
Dm Fm C D7 D G7 G C
You are too beau-ti - ful and I am a fool for beau - ty.

You Belong to Me

Registration 4
Rhythm: Ballad

Words and Music by Pee Wee King,
Redd Stewart and Chilton Price

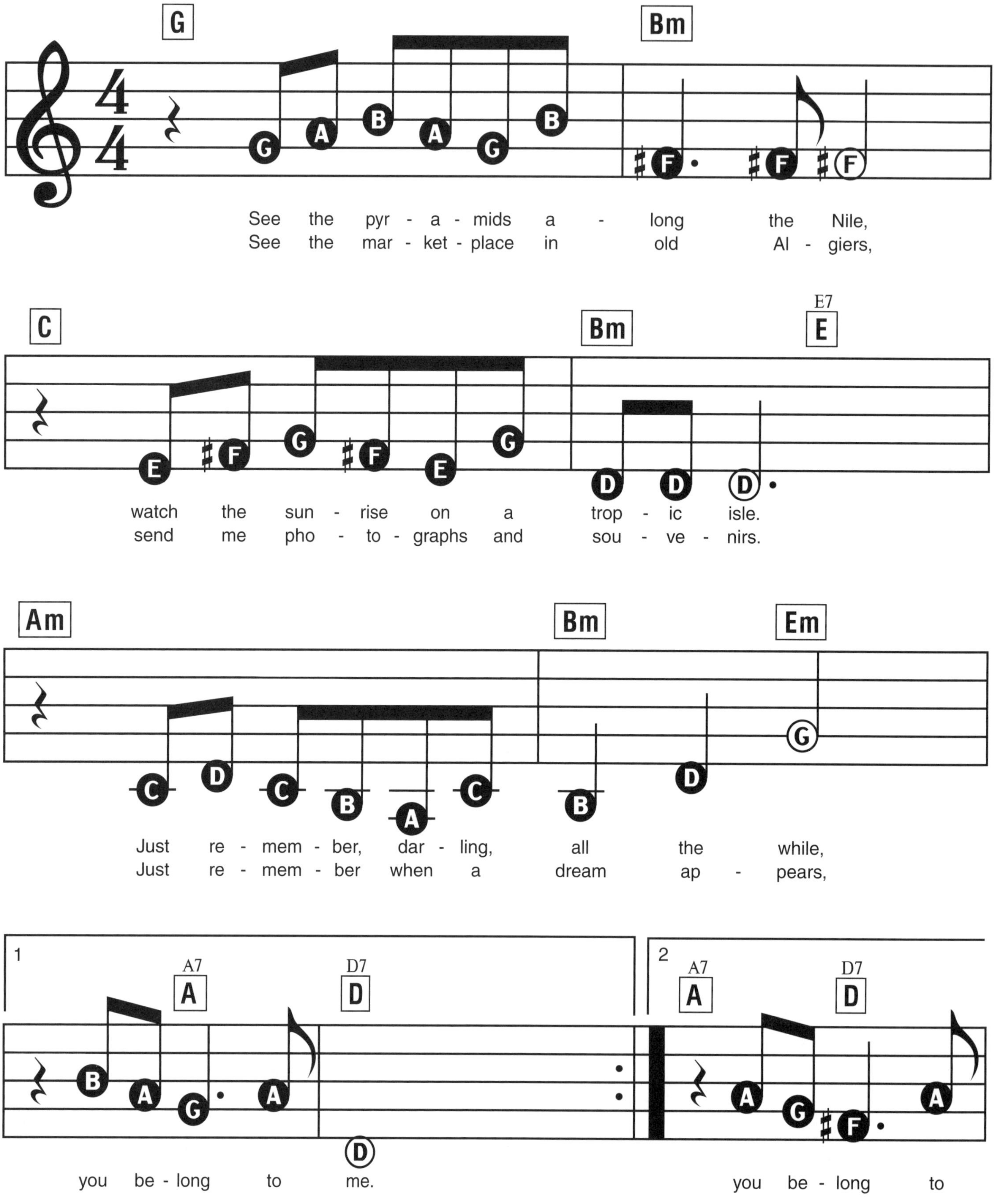
G
Bm
See the pyr - a - mids a - long the Nile,
See the mar - ket - place in old Al - giers,
C
Bm
E7
E
watch the sun - rise on a trop - ic isle.
send me pho - to - graphs and sou - ve - nirs.
Am
Bm
Em
Just re - mem - ber, dar - ling, all the while,
Just re - mem - ber when a dream ap - pears,
1
A7
A
D7
D
you be - long to me.
2
A7
A
D7
D
you be - long to

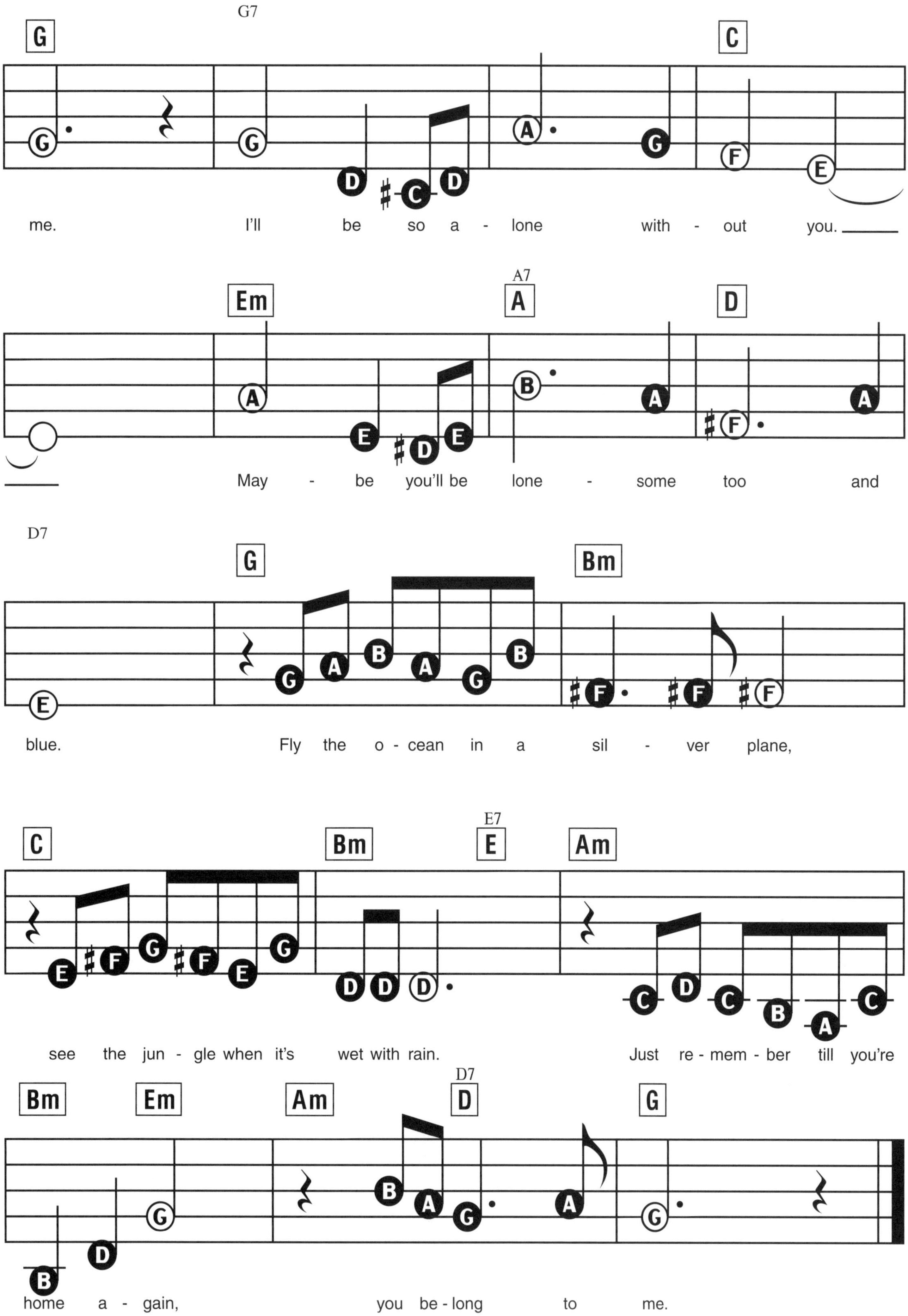
G
G7
C
me. I'll be so a - lone with - out you.
Em
A7
A
D
May - be you'll be lone - some too and
D7
G
Bm
blue. Fly the o - cean in a sil - ver plane,
C
Bm
E7
E
Am
see the jun - gle when it's wet with rain. Just re - mem - ber till you're
Bm
Em
Am
D7
D
G
home a - gain, you be - long to me.

You're in My Heart

Registration 1
Rhythm: Shuffle or Swing

Words and Music by
Rod Stewart

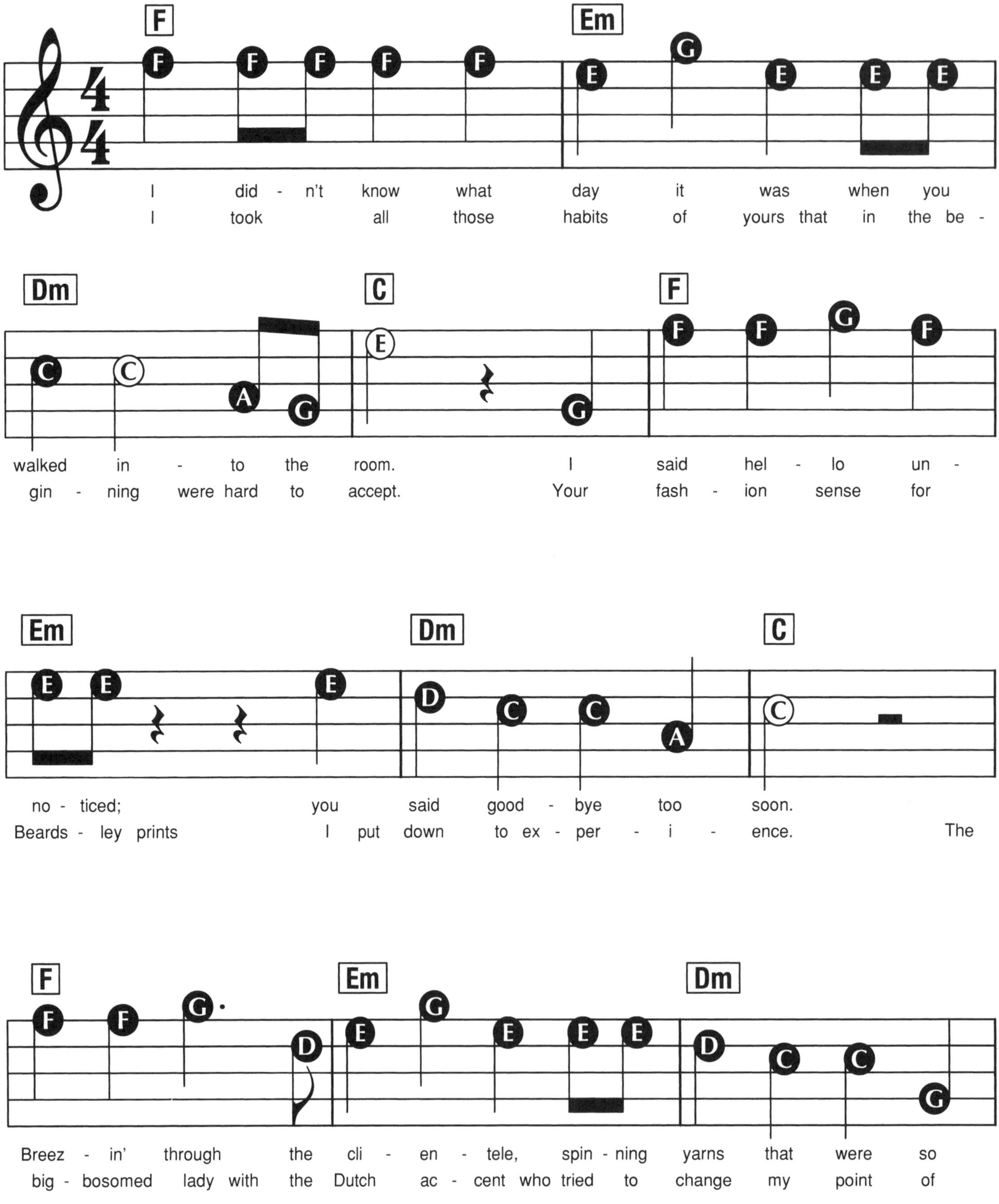
F Em
I did - n't know what day it was when you
I took all those habits of yours that in the be -
Dm C F
walked in - to the room. I said hel - lo un -
gin - ning were hard to accept. Your fash - ion sense for
Em Dm C
no - ticed; you said good - bye too soon.
Beards - ley prints I put down to ex - per - i - ence. The
F Em Dm
Breez - in' through the cli - en - tele, spin - ning yarns that were so
big - bosomed lady with the Dutch ac - cent who tried to change my point of

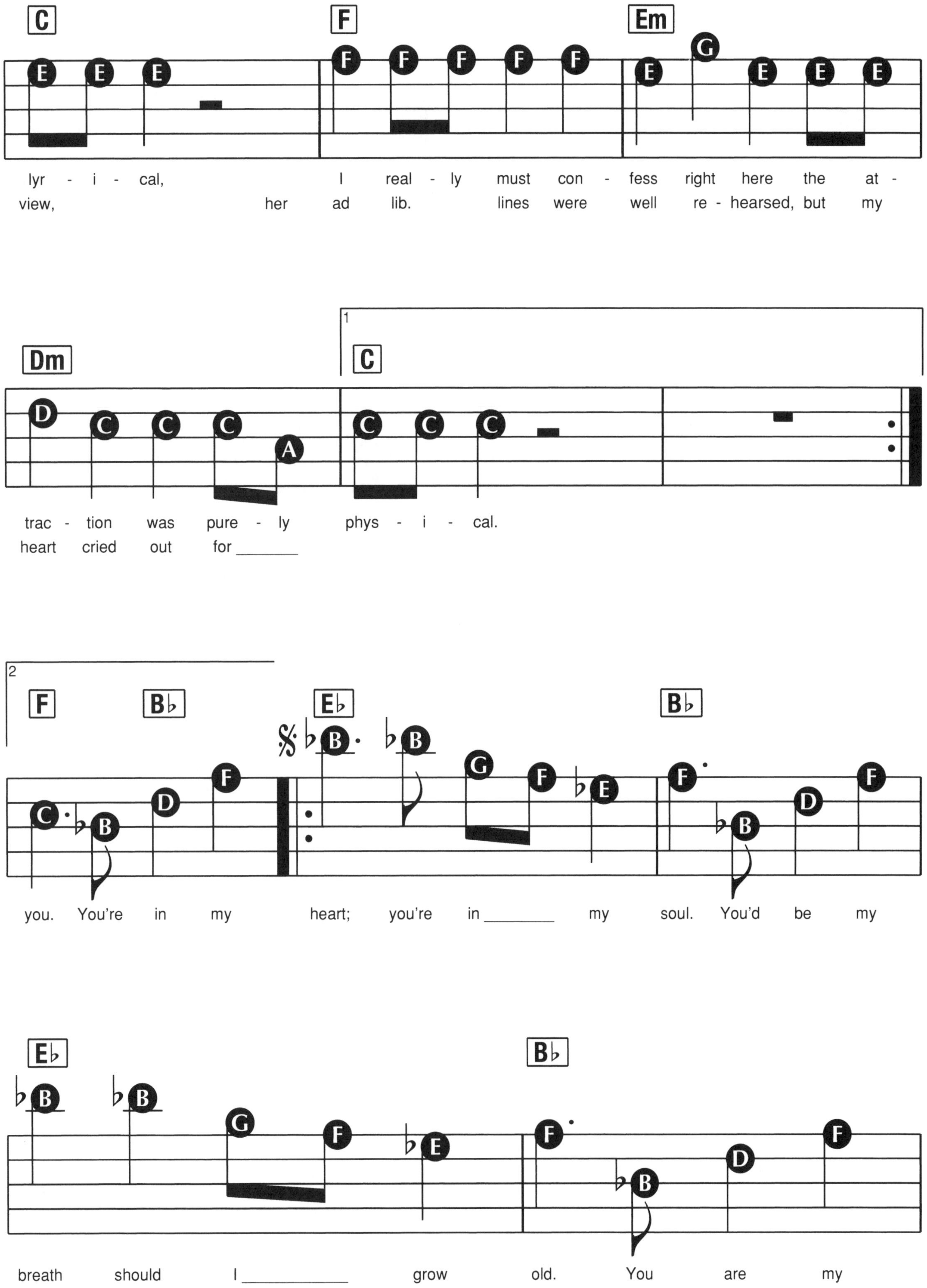
C F Em
lyr - i - cal, I real - ly must con - fess right here the at -
view, her ad lib. lines were well re - hearsed, but my
Dm 1 C
trac - tion was pure - ly phys - i - cal.
heart cried out for
2 F B♭ E♭ B♭
you. You're in my heart; you're in my soul. You'd be my
E♭ B♭
breath should I grow old. You are my

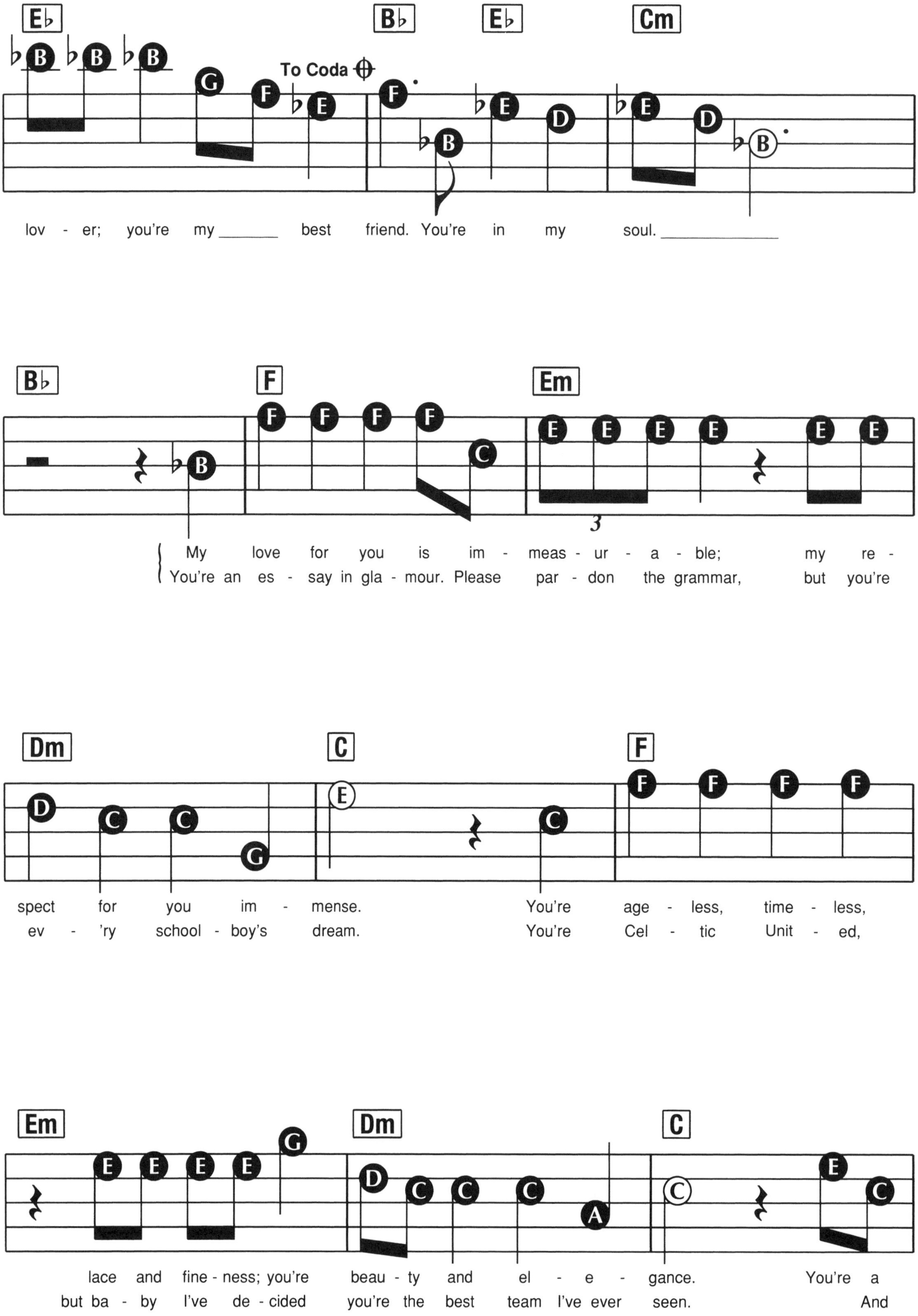
E♭ B♭ E♭ Cm
To Coda
lov - er; you're my best friend. You're in my soul.
B♭ F Em
My love for you is im - meas - ur - a - ble; my re -
You're an es - say in gla - mour. Please par - don the grammar, but you're
Dm C F
spect for you im - mense. You're age - less, time - less,
ev - 'ry school - boy's dream. You're Cel - tic Unit - ed,
Em Dm C
lace and fine - ness; you're beau - ty and el - e - gance. You're a
but ba - by I've de - cided you're the best team I've ever seen. And

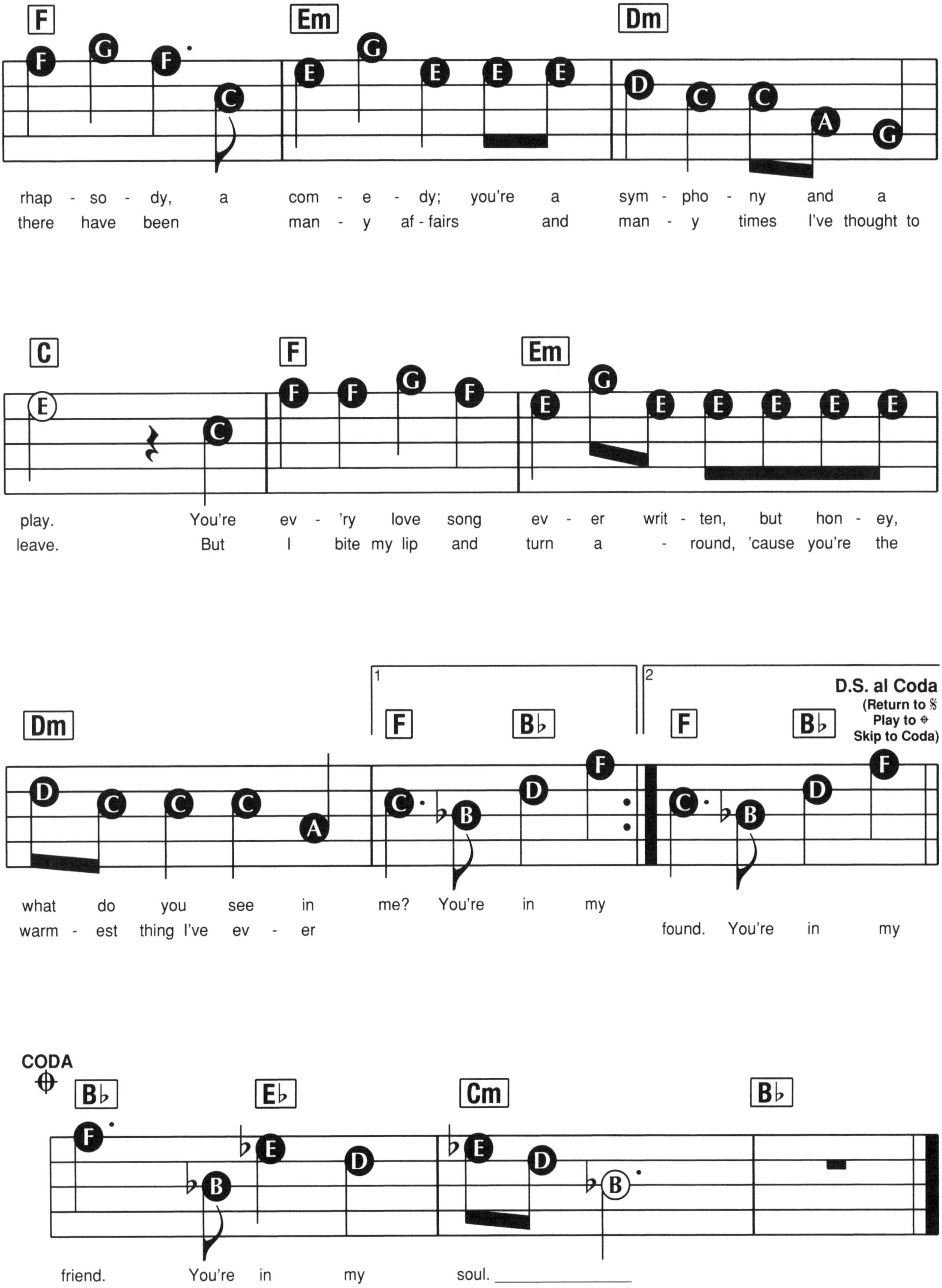
F Em Dm
rhap - so - dy, a com - e - dy; you're a sym - pho - ny and a
there have been man - y af - fairs and man - y times I've thought to
C F Em
play. You're ev - 'ry love song ev - er writ - ten, but hon - ey,
leave. But I bite my lip and turn a - round, 'cause you're the
Dm
1 F B♭
2 F B♭
D.S. al Coda
(Return to 𝄋
Play to 𝄌
Skip to Coda)
what do you see in me? You're in my
warm - est thing I've ev - er found. You're in my
CODA
B♭ E♭ Cm B♭
friend. You're in my soul.

Three Times a Lady

Registration 1
Rhythm: Waltz

Words and Music by
Lionel Richie

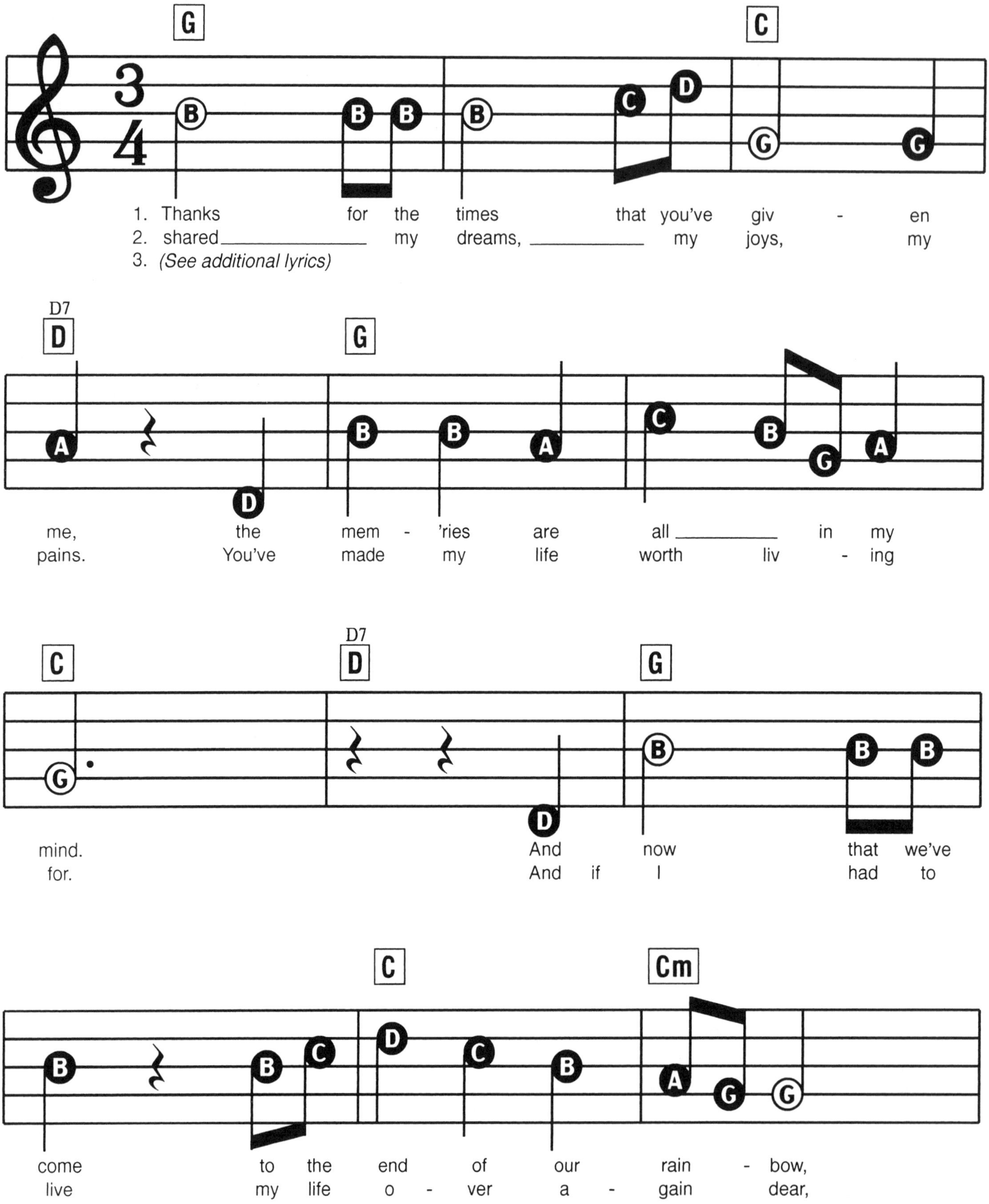
G
C
1. Thanks for the times that you've giv - en
2. shared ____ my dreams, ____ my joys, my
3. (See additional lyrics)
D7
D
G
me, the mem - 'ries are all ____ in my
pains. You've made my life worth liv - ing
C
D7
D
G
mind. And now that we've
for. And if I had to
C
Cm
come to the end of our rain - bow,
live my life o - ver a - gain dear,

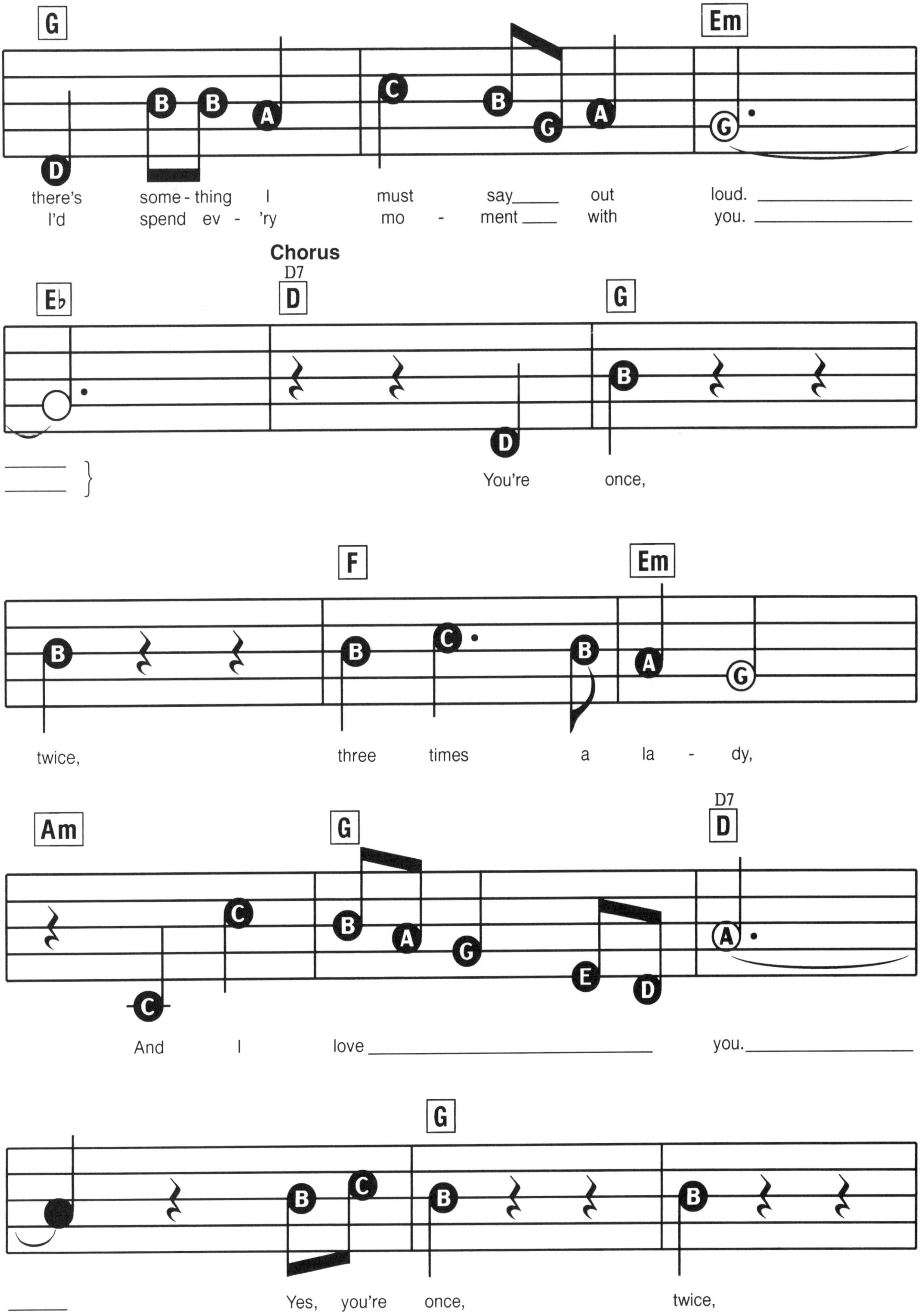
G
Em
D
B
B
A
C
B
G
A
G
there's some - thing I must say out loud.
I'd spend ev - 'ry mo - ment with you.
Chorus
D7
E♭
D
G
D
B
You're once,
F
Em
B
B
C
B
A
G
twice, three times a la - dy,
Am
G
D7
D
C
C
B
A
G
E
D
A
And I love you.
G
B
C
B
B
Yes, you're once, twice,

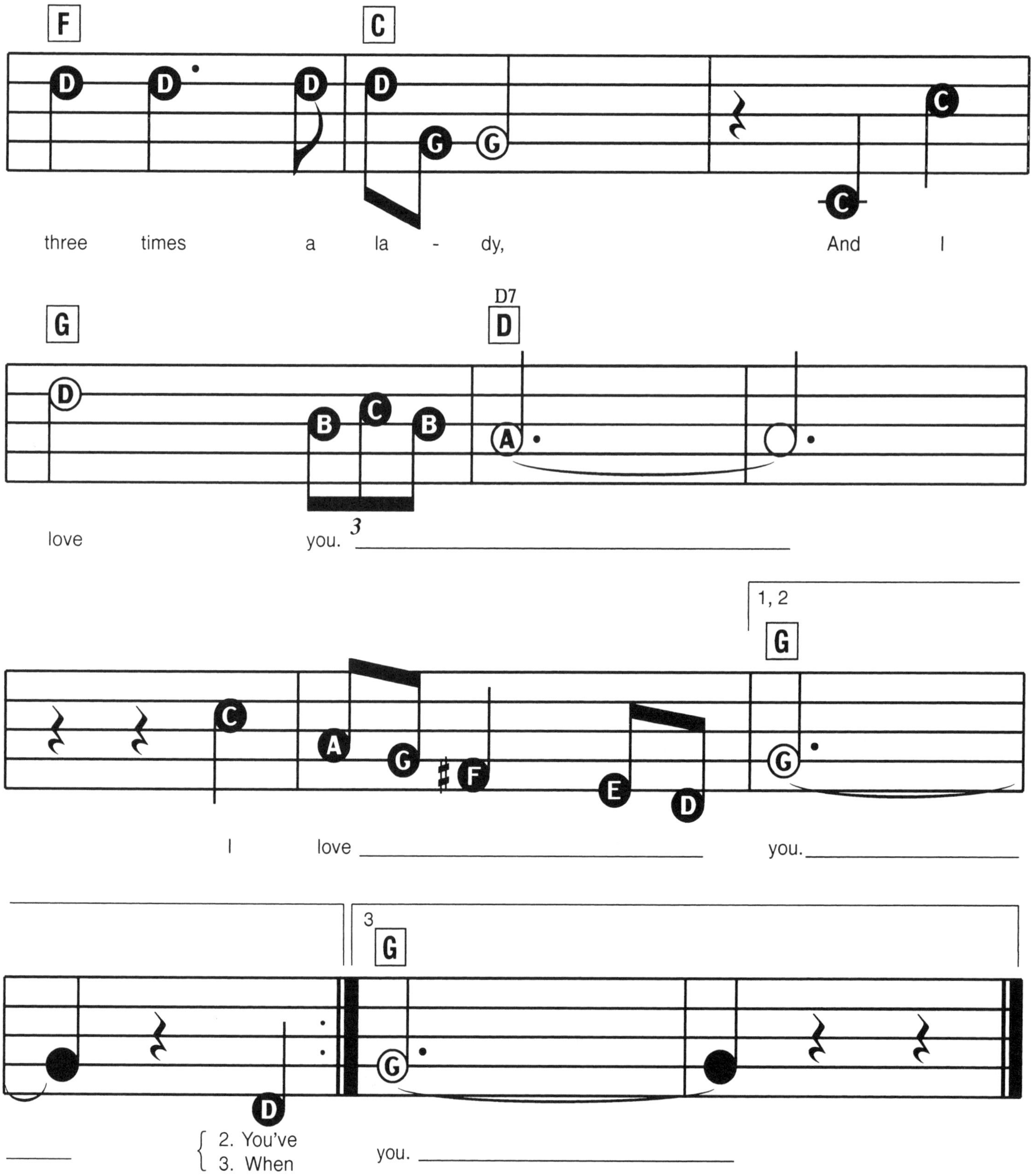
F
C
three times a la - dy,
And I
G
D7
D
love you.
3
1, 2
G
I love you.
2. You've
3. When
3
G
you.

Additional Lyrics

3. When we are together the moments I cherish
With ev'ry beat of my heart.
To touch you, to hold you, to feel you, to need you.
There's nothing to keep us apart.
Chorus

E-Z Play Today Registration Guide

- Match the Registration number on the song to the corresponding numbered category below. Select and activate an instrumental sound available on your instrument.
- Choose an automatic rhythm appropriate to the mood and style of the song. (Consult your Owner's Guide for proper operation of automatic rhythm features.)
- Adjust the tempo and volume controls to comfortable settings.

Registration

1	Mellow	Flutes, Clarinet, Oboe, Flugel Horn, Trombone, French Horn, Organ Flutes
2	Ensemble	Brass Section, Sax Section, Wind Ensemble, Full Organ, Theater Organ
3	Strings	Violin, Viola, Cello, Fiddle, String Ensemble, Pizzicato, Organ Strings
4	Guitars	Acoustic/Electric Guitars, Banjo, Mandolin, Dulcimer, Ukulele, Hawaiian Guitar
5	Mallets	Vibraphone, Marimba, Xylophone, Steel Drums, Bells, Celesta, Chimes
6	Liturgical	Pipe Organ, Hand Bells, Vocal Ensemble, Choir, Organ Flutes
7	Bright	Saxophones, Trumpet, Mute Trumpet, Synth Leads, Jazz/Gospel Organs
8	Piano	Piano, Electric Piano, Honky Tonk Piano, Harpsichord, Clavi
9	Novelty	Melodic Percussion, Wah Trumpet, Synth, Whistle, Kazoo, Perc. Organ
10	Bellows	Accordion, French Accordion, Mussette, Harmonica, Pump Organ, Bagpipes